Pocket
BUDAPEST
TOP SIGHTS • LOCAL LIFE • MADE EASY

Steve Fallon, Anna Kaminski

In This Book

QuickStart Guide

Your keys to understanding the city – we help you decide what to do and how to do it

Need to Know
Tips for a smooth trip

Neighbourhoods
What's where

Explore Budapest

The best things to see and do, neighbourhood by neighbourhood

Top Sights
Make the most of your visit

Local Life
The insider's city

The Best of Budapest

The city's highlights in handy lists to help you plan

Best Walks
See the city on foot

Budapest's Best...
The best experiences

Survival Guide

Tips and tricks for a seamless, hassle-free city experience

Getting Around
Travel like a local

Essential Information
Including where to stay

Our selection of the city's best places to eat, drink and experience:

◉ **Sights**

✖ **Eating**

🍷 **Drinking**

✪ **Entertainment**

🔒 **Shopping**

These symbols give you the vital information for each listing:

- 📞 Telephone Numbers
- ⊙ Opening Hours
- 🅿 Parking
- 🚭 Nonsmoking
- @ Internet Access
- 📶 Wi-Fi Access
- 🌱 Vegetarian Selection
- 📖 English-Language Menu
- 👶 Family-Friendly
- 🐾 Pet-Friendly
- 🚌 Bus
- ⛴ Ferry
- Ⓜ Metro
- Ⓢ Subway
- 🚋 Tram
- 🚆 Train

Find each listing quickly on maps for each neighbourhood:

Bar Hemingway

16 🍷 Map p233, B2

Legend has it that Hemi self, wielding a machine rate this timber-pan ered bar during showpiece is a en by Papa ar town. Dress s.com; Hôtel Rit ⊙6.30pm-2a

6 ◉ Plac

Lonely Planet's Budapest

Lonely Planet Pocket Guides are designed to get you straight to the heart of the city.

Inside you'll find all the must-see sights, plus tips to make your visit to each one really memorable. We've split the city into easy-to-navigate neighbourhoods and provided clear maps so you'll find your way around with ease. Our expert authors have searched out the best of the city: walks, food, nightlife and shopping, to name a few. Because you want to explore, our 'Local Life' pages will take you to some of the most exciting areas to experience the real Budapest.

And of course you'll find all the practical tips you need for a smooth trip: itineraries for short visits, how to get around, and how much to tip the guy who serves you a drink at the end of a long day's exploration.

It's your guarantee of a really great experience.

Our Promise

You can trust our travel information because Lonely Planet authors visit the places we write about, each and every edition. We never accept freebies for positive coverage, so you can rely on us to tell it like it is.

QuickStart Guide **7**

Explore Budapest **21**

Worth a Trip:

The Best of Budapest 123

Budapest's Best Walks

Budapest's Best ...

Survival Guide 145

QuickStart Guide

Welcome to Budapest

Straddling the Danube with the Buda Hills as backdrop and boasting enough baroque, neoclassical and art nouveau architecture to satisfy anyone, Budapest is plentifully endowed with natural and human-made beauty. But the Queen of the Danube is not just a pretty face. At night she frocks up to become what is now the region's premier party town.

Szechenyi Baths (p119)
LI KIM GOH/GETTY IMAGES ©

Budapest
Top Sights

Royal Palace (p24)

The focal point of Castle Hill in Buda and the city's most visited sight, the enormous Royal Palace contains two important museums, the national library and an abundance of notable statues and monuments.

Gellért Baths (p38)

'Taking the waters' is very much a part of everyday life in Budapest and soaking in the art nouveau Gellért Baths, with temperatures of up to 38°C, has been likened to bathing in a cathedral.

Basilica of St Stephen (p76)

Budapest's most important Christian house of worship is a gem of neoclassical architecture and contains the nation's most sacred object: the holy right hand of King St Stephen.

Hungarian National Museum (p110)

Purpose-built in 1847, this museum houses the nation's most important collection of historical relics, from King Stephen's crimson silk coronation mantle to memorabilia from socialist times.

JULIE MAYFENG/SHUTTERSTOCK ©

PH FERDINANDO SCAVONE/GETTY IMAGES ©

Parliament (p74)

The centrepiece along the Danube in Pest and Hungary's largest building, Parliament is the seat of the National Assembly and contains the coronation regalia of King Stephen.

Citadella & Liberty Monument (p40)

Built after the War of Independence, the Citadella atop Gellért Hill is a fortress that never saw battle. Nearby is Liberty Monument, the lovely lady with a palm frond proclaiming freedom throughout the city.

Memento Park (p48)

Containing garish statues and over-the-top memorials from the Communist period, Memento Park could be described as both a cemetery of socialist mistakes and a well-manicured trash heap of history.

Aquincum (p58)

Today's Budapest was settled by the Romans at the end of the 1st century AD and Aquincum, the most complete civilian Roman town in Hungary, now contains an enclosed museum and an open-air archaeological park.

ESTEA/SHUTTERSTOCK ©

CHRISDORNEY/SHUTTERSTOCK ©

City Park (p118)

Pest's green lung, City Park is an open space measuring almost exactly a square kilometre and contains museums, galleries, a zoo, a permanent circus and one of the best thermal baths in the city.

Great Synagogue (p94)

The largest Jewish temple in Europe, the Moorish-style Great Synagogue with its iconic copper dome is one of Budapest's most eye-catching and beloved buildings.

Budapest Local Life

Local experiences and hidden gems to help you uncover the real city

After taking in Budapest's fabulous array of sights, it's time to get behind what everyone sees in order to discover the Budapest local people know and love: the superb restaurants, the quirky shops and markets, and the bars and clubs that never say die.

Touring the Buda Hills (p60)

▶ Clear air

▶ Quirky transport

They may be short on sights, but the Buda Hills are a welcome respite from the hot, dusty city in summer. Perhaps their biggest draws are their unusual forms of transport: a 19th-century narrow-gauge cog railway, a train run by children and a chairlift that will get you back down to terra firma.

Bar-Hopping in Erzsébetváros (p96)

▶ Craft beers

▶ World-class wine

Don't just follow the herd when day becomes night in this super party town. We have the low-down on where's the most fun with the least amount of hassle in the very heart of the nightlife area: Erzsébetváros.

Exploring Váci utca & Vörösmarty tér (p64)

▶ Top shops

▶ Beckoning cafes

Follow us on a walking tour of Budapest's premier shopping street that eschews the chain stores and brand-name shops in favour of more upscale local emporiums, notable buildings and smart cafes, including the iconic Gerbeaud, the capital's finest *cukrászda* (cake shop).

From Market to Market in Southern Pest (p112)

▶ Local specialities

▶ Living history

In this tale of two markets – one a visitor's paradise, the other where auntie shops – we walk the backstreets, discovering everything from antiquarian bookshops and cool cafes to ghosts of the 1956 Uprising that still haunt the neighbourhood.

Cog Railway, Buda Hills

Szimpla Farmers Market

Other great places to experience the city like a local:

Szimpla Farmers Market (p106)

Fortuna Önkiszolgáló (p32)

Károly Garden (p70)

Pump Room (p46)

Laci! Konyha! (p89)

BÁV (p83)

Pintér Galéria (p83)

Budapest Day Planner

Day One

Spend your first morning in Budapest on Castle Hill, taking in the views from the **Royal Palace** (p24) and establishing the lay of the land. There are museums aplenty up here, but don't be greedy: you only have time for one. We recommend either the **Hungarian National Gallery** (p25) for fine Hungarian art or the rebranded **Castle Museum** (p27) for a seamless introduction to the city's long and tortuous past. Grab a quick lunch at **Fortuna Önkiszolgáló** (p32) or try some Hungarian classics at **Mandragóra** (p32).

In the afternoon ride the **Siklό** (p25) down to Clark Ádám tér and make your way up Fő utca to the **Király Baths** (p31) for a relaxing soak.

Depending on your mood, check to see what's on at the **Budavár Cultural Centre** (p34) or head for stylish **Oscar American Bar** (p34) for cocktails and canned music.

Day Two

On your second day, cross the Danube and see Pest at its very finest by walking up leafy **Andrássy út** (p100), which will take you on your way to Heroes' Sq, past the architectural gem the **Hungarian State Opera House** (p80), and wonderful cafes including **Spinoza Café** (p103) and **Lotz Terem Book Cafe** (p104).

As you approach City Park, decide whether you want an educational or leisurely afternoon (or both). The **House of Terror** (p100) is on Andrássy út, and on the east side of Heroes' Sq is the **Palace of Art** (p121), with excellent exhibitions. City Park contains the **Budapest Zoo** (p121) and the wonderful **Széchenyi Baths** (p119).

Settle in for dinner at the informal but stylish **Robinson** (p119); in the warmer months, try for a table on the lakeside terrace. If you're keen to kick on after dinner, head to the lively streets in Erzsébetváros and the Jewish Quarter.

hort on time?
e've arranged Budapest's must-sees into these day-by-day itineraries to make sure
ou see the very best of the city in the time you have available.

ay Three

☼ On day three it's time to see a few of Budapest's big-ticket attractions. In the morning concentrate on the wo icons of Hungarian nationhood and he places that house them: the Crown f St Stephen in the **Parliament** (p74) uilding and the saint-king's mortal emains (just a hand) in the **Basilica of t Stephen** (p76). To get from one to he other cut through Szabadság tér and ave a glance at the last remaining Soviet nemorial in the city.

☼ In the afternoon explore the Jewish Quarter, with a neighbourhood alk taking in such sights as Klauzál tér, he **Orthodox Synagogue** (p101) and he original ghetto wall. Make sure you ave ample time for a good look inside he **Great Synagogue** (p94) and the **lungarian Jewish Museum & Archives** p95), and have a slice of something sweet t the **Fröhlich Cukrászda** (p95) kosher ake shop.

☾ If it's Friday there will be *klezmer* (Jewish folk music) at **Spinoza afé** (p103). Afterwards move on to the realth of *kertek* ('garden clubs') along azinczy utca: try **Mika Tivadar Mulató** p105) or the grandaddy of them all, szimpla Kert** (p103) or, for a candlelight ibe, try **Doblo** (p103) wine bar.

Day Four

☼ On your last day have a look at what the west side of the Danube used to be like by strolling through Óbuda and learning how Buda, Óbuda and Pest all came together. Again, the choice of museums and attractions is legion, but the **Vasarely Museum** (p54) and its hallucinogenic works never fail to please, and the nearby **Hungarian Museum of Trade & Tourism** (p55) is a positive delight. Alternatively, **Aquincum** (p58) is a short HÉV ride away.

☼ In the afternoon, head south for **Margaret Bridge** (p87). Just up the hill to the west is **Gül Baba's Tomb** (p54), the only Muslim place of pilgrimage in northern Europe still in existence. Spend the rest of the afternoon pampering yourself at the wonderful **Veli Bej Baths** (p54).

☾ Cross over the bridge for a home-style dinner at **Firkász** (p90), followed up with some sophisticated jazz at the **Budapest Jazz Club** (p91).

Need to Know

For more information,
see Survival Guide (p145)

Currency
Hungarian forint (Ft); some hotels quote in euros (€)

Language
Hungarian (Magyar)

Visas
Generally not required for stays up to 90 days.

Money
ATMs are everywhere. Visa, MasterCard and American Express widely accepted in many hotels and restaurants.

Mobile Phones
Local SIM cards can be used in European and Australian phones, as well as most North American ones.

Time
Central European Time (GMT/UTC plus one hour)

Plugs & Adaptors
Plugs have two round pins; electrical current is 230V/50Hz.

Tipping
Hungarians are very tip-conscious and nearly everyone in Budapest will routinely hand gratuities to waiters, hairdressers and taxi drivers.

① Before You Go

Your Daily Budget

Budget Less than 15,000Ft
► Dorm bed 3000–6500Ft
► Meal at self-service restaurant 1500Ft
► Three-day transport pass 4150Ft

Midrange 15,000–35,000Ft
► Single/double room from 7500/10,000Ft
► Two-course meal with drink 3500–7500Ft
► Cocktail from 1500Ft

Top End more than 35,000Ft
► Double in superior hotel from 16,500Ft
► Dinner for two with wine from 12,500Ft
► Spa ticket adult/child 3600/1600Ft
► Cover charge at popular club 1500–2500Ft

Useful Websites

Budapest Info (www.budapestinfo.hu) One of the better overall tourist websites.

Budapest by Locals (www.budapestbylocals. com) Excellent and very useful expat-driven site full of both glaringly obvious information that impress even us.

Lonely Planet (www.lonelyplanet.com/ budapest) Destination information, hotel bookings, traveller forum and more.

Advance Planning

Two months before Book accommodation if travelling in high season. Check 'what's on' and English-language media websites.

One month before Reserve seats for big-ticket concerts, musical or dance performances; book top-end restaurants.

One week before Ensure your bookings are in order and you have all booking references.

2 Arriving in Budapest

ost people arrive in Budapest by air, but you
an also get here from dozens of European
ties by bus and train and from Vienna by
anube hydrofoil.

✈ From Ferenc Liszt International
irport

inibuses, buses and trains to central
udapest run from 4am to midnight; taxis
st from 6000Ft. The cheapest (and most
me-consuming) way to get into the city
entre is to take bus 200E (350Ft; on the bus
50Ft) – look for the stop on the footpath
etween terminals 2A and 2B – which
rminates at the Kőbánya-Kispest metro
tation. From there take the M3 metro into
e city centre. The total cost is 700Ft.
Between midnight and 4am night bus
00 makes the run.

⎕ From Keleti, Nyugati & Déli Train
stations

ll three are connected to metro lines of the
ame name and night buses call when the
etro is closed.

⎕ From Népliget & Stadion Bus
stations

oth stations are on metro lines (M2 and M3
espectively) which go to Deák tér, and are
erved by trams 1 and 1A.

⛴ From International Ferry Pier

ienna hydrofoils arrive at and depart from
he International Ferry Pier, which is between
izabeth and Liberty Bridges on the Pest
de. It's on tram line 2 and close to the
vám tér station of the M4 metro line.

3 Getting Around

Budapest has a safe, efficient and inexpensive public-transport system. Five types of
transport are in general use, but the most
relevant for travellers are the metro trains on
four numbered and colour-coded city lines,
blue buses and yellow trams. The basic fare
for all forms of transport is 350Ft (3000Ft
for a block of 10) allowing you to travel as far
as you like on the same metro, bus, trolleybus
or tram line without changing/transferring.

Ⓜ Metro

Budapest has four underground metro lines.
The M1, M2 and M3 converge at Pest's central
Deák Ferenc tér (only), while the M4 links
to the M2 at Keleti train station and the M3
at Kálvin tér, both in Pest. The M2 reaches
central Széll Kálmán tér in Buda; the M4
serves south Buda. All four metro lines run
from about 4am and begin their last journey
at around 11.15pm.

🚌 Bus

An extensive network of regular buses runs
from around 4.15am to between 9pm and
11.30pm; from 11.30pm to just after 4am a
network of 41 night buses (indicated by three
digits beginning with '9') kicks in.

🚋 Tram

Faster and more pleasant for sightseeing
than buses; a network of 30 lines. Tram 6
runs overnight.

🚗 Taxi

Taxis in Budapest are cheap by European
standards, and are – at long last – fully
regulated, with uniform flag-fall (450Ft) and
per-kilometre charges (280Ft).

Budapest
Neighbourhoods

Óbuda (p50)

This is the oldest part of Buda and retains a lost-in-the-past village feel; here you'll find the remains of the Roman settlement of Aquincum and some legendary eateries.

Castle District (p22)

Castle Hill, nerve centre of Budapest's history and packed with important museums, is here, as is ground-level Víziváros, with some excellent restaurants.

◉ Top Sights

Royal Palace

Gellért Hill & Tabán (p36)

The Citadella and the Liberty Monument gaze down from atop Gellért Hill on the neighbourhood of the Tabán.

◉ Top Sights

Citadella & Liberty Monument

Gellért Baths

Parliame

Royal Palace ◉

Citadell
Liberty
Monume
◉

Margaret Island & Northern Pest (p84)

This unspoiled island in the Danube offers a green refuge, while northern Pest beckons with its shops and lovely cafes.

Parliament & Around (p72)

Takes in the areas around the Parliament building and the equally iconic Basilica of St Stephen, plus Nagymező utca, Budapest's Broadway.

⊙ Top Sights

Parliament

Basilica of St Stephen

⊙ *City Park*

Erzsébetváros & the Jewish Quarter (p92)

This neighbourhood offers the lion's share of Budapest's accommodation, restaurants serving every cuisine under the sun and the city's hottest nightspots.

⊙ Top Sights

Great Synagogue

Worth a Trip

⊙ Top Sights

Memento Park (p48)

Aquincum (p58)

Buda Hills (p60)

City Park (p118)

⊙ *Basilica of St Stephen*

⊙ *Great Synagogue*

⊙ *Hungarian National Museum*

Southern Pest (p108)

Traditionally working class, this is an area to wander, poking your nose into courtyards and small, often traditional, shops.

⊙ Top Sights

Hungarian National Museum

llért
ths

Belváros (p62)

The 'Inner Town' centres on touristy Váci utca, with its shops and bars, and Vörösmarty tér, home to the city's most celebrated *cukrászda* (cake shop).

Explore
Budapest

Worth a Trip

Cityscape of Budapest
TEEMU TRETJAKOV/500PX ©

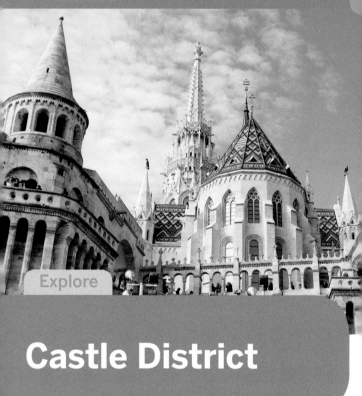

Explore

Castle District

Castle Hill (Várhegy) is a 1km-long limestone plateau towering 170m above the Danube. The premier sight in the capital, it contains Budapest's most important medieval monuments and museums in two distinct areas: the Old Town and the Royal Palace. Víziváros (Watertown) is the narrow area between the Danube and Castle Hill that spreads as far as Széll Kálmán tér, Buda's most important transport hub.

The Sights in a Day

☀ You could spend an entire day or even longer on Castle Hill given the wealth of attractions here, but try to restrain yourself. Make your way up on the **Sikló** (p25) and choose either the **Hungarian National Gallery** (p25) or **Castle Museum** (p27). Then walk over to the **Fishermen's Bastion** (p30) to enjoy the views and peek inside **Matthias Church** (p30).

☀ For lunch, nab a table at the family-run **Mandragóra** (p32). Afterward, walk over to the **Hospital in the Rock** (p31) and join a tour of the underground passages. Next for something lighter, educate yourself on the development of Budapest's musical history at the **Music History Museum** (p30).

☽ In the late afternoon walk through Vienna Gate to **Oscar American Bar** (p34) for a libation. One of our favourite restaurants, **Csalogány 26** (p32), is within easy striking distance. And check out what's on at the **Budavár Cultural Centre** (p34) for later. If you're lucky a *táncház* (folk music and dance) session will be on the program.

 Top Sights

Royal Palace (p24)

❤ **Best of Budapest**

Eating

Csalogány 26 (p32)

Fortuna Önkiszolgáló (p32)

Drinking

Kávé Műhely (p33)

Ruszwurm Cukrászda (p33)

Oscar American Bar (p34)

Museums & Galleries

Hungarian National Gallery (p25)

Castle Museum (p27)

Music History Museum (p30)

Getting There

🚌 **Bus** I Clark Ádám tér or V Deák Ferenc tér in Pest for 16 to I Dísz tér on Castle Hill.

🚟 **Funicular** I Clark Ádám tér for Sikló to I Szent György tér on Castle Hill.

🚈 **HÉV** Batthyány tér.

Ⓜ **Metro** M2 Batthyány tér and Széll Kálmán tér.

🚋 **Tram** II Vidra utca for 17 to Óbuda; I Batthyány tér for 19 to I Szent Gellért tér and south Buda; 4 and 6 to Pest (Big Ring Rd).

Top Sights
Royal Palace

The enormous Royal Palace has been razed and rebuilt six times over the past seven centuries. Béla IV established a residence here in the mid-13th century and subsequent kings added to it. The palace was levelled in the battle to rout the Turks in 1686. Today it contains two important museums and numerous statues and monuments.

Királyi Palota

⊙ Map p28, E8

I Szent György tér

🚌 16, 16A, 116

Ornamental Entrances

There are three ways to enter the palace. The first is via the Habsburg Steps and through an ornamental gateway dating from 1903. The second way is via Corvinus Gate, with its big black raven symbolising King Matthias Corvinus. Either is good for the museums. Finally, you can take the escalator or steps from the Garden Bazaar below the south end of Castle Hill.

Hungarian National Gallery

The **Hungarian National Gallery** (Nemzeti Galéria; 📱1-201 9082; www.mng.hu; I Szent György tér 2, Bldgs A–D; adult/concession 1800/900Ft; audio guide 1000Ft; ⏰10am-6pm Tue-Sun) spreads across four floors that traces Hungarian art from the 11th century to the present day. The largest collections include medieval and Renaissance stonework, Gothic wooden sculptures and panel paintings, late Gothic winged altars and late Renaissance and baroque art. The museum also has an important collection of 19th- and 20th-century art.

Gothic Works

The winged altarpieces in the so-called Great Throne Room (1st floor, Building D) date from the 15th and early 16th centuries and form one of the greatest collections of late Gothic painting in the world. The almost modern *Visitation* (1506) by Master MS is both lyrical and intimate, but keep an eye open for the intense, almost Renaissance face of John the Baptist in a series of four paintings (1490) of scenes from his life.

Renaissance & Baroque Works

The finest 18th-century baroque painters in Hungary were actually Austrians, including Franz Anton Maulbertsch (1724–96; *Death of St Joseph*) and his contemporary Stephan Dorfmeister (1725–97; *Christ on the Cross*). You'll find their

☑ Top Tips

▶ The most fun way to reach Castle Hill is by boarding the **Sikló** (II Hunyadi János út; one-way/return adult 1200/1800Ft, 6-26yr 700/1100Ft; ⏰7.30am-10pm), a funicular railway built in 1870 that ascends from Clark Ádám tér at the western end of Chain Bridge to Szent György tér near the Royal Palace.

▶ Catch the low-key but ceremonial changing of the guard at the nearby Sándor Palace hourly between 9am and 5pm.

▶ If you want to leave Castle Hill after visiting the Castle Museum, exiting through the museum's back courtyard door will take you straight down to I Szarvas tér in Tabán.

✗ Take a Break

If you want something hot and/or sweet after your visit to the museum(s), head for Ruszwurm Cukrászda (p33) or stop by Pierrot (p33) for a drink in refined surroundings.

works in the galleries adjoining the Great Throne Room on the 1st floor.

19th-Century Works

Building C contains examples of the National Romantic School of paintings: *Women of Eger* by Bertalan Székely (1835–1910) and *The Baptism of Vajk* by Gyula Benczúr (1844–1920). In Building B are works by the 'painter of the Great Plain', Mihály Munkácsy (1844–1900; *Storm in the Puszta*), and by the impressionist Pál Szinyei Merse (1845–1920; *The Skylark*).

20th-Century Works

Two greats working in the late 19th and early 20th centuries were Tivadar Kosztka Csontváry (1853–1919) and József Rippl-Rónai (1861–1927; *Father and Uncle Piacsek Drinking Red Wine*). The harrowing depictions of war by László Mednyánszky (1852–1919; *In Serbia*) and the colourful works of Vilmos Aba-Novák (1894–1941; *The Fair at Csikszereda*) are also in Building C, 2nd floor.

HUNGARIAN NATIONAL GALLERY

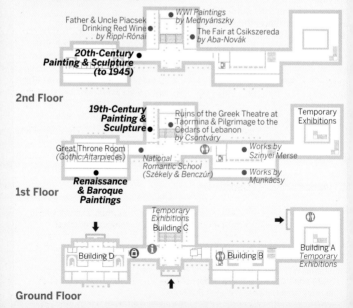

Castle Museum

The **Castle Museum** (Vármúzeum; ☎1-487 8800; www.btm.hu; I Szent György tér 2, Bldg E; adult/concession 2000/1000Ft; ⊙10am-6pm Tue-Sun Mar-Oct, to 4pm Nov-Feb) explores the city's 2000-year history over three floors. Restored palace rooms dating from the 15th century can be entered from the basement, where there are three vaulted halls. One of the halls features a magnificent Renaissance door frame in red marble bearing the seal of Queen Beatrix and tiles with a raven and a ring (the seal of her husband, King Matthias Corvinus), leading to the Gothic and Renaissance Halls, the Royal Cellar and the vaulted Tower Chapel (1320) dedicated to St Stephen.

National Széchenyi Library

The **National Széchenyi Library** (Országos Széchenyi Könyvtár; ☎1-224 3700; www.oszk.hu; I Szent György tér 4-6, Bldg F; ⊙9am-8pm, stacks to 7pm Tue-Sat) contains a large collection of codices and manuscripts, a large collection of foreign newspapers and a copy of everything published in Hungary or the Hungarian language. It was founded in 1802 by Count Ferenc Széchenyi, who endowed it with 15,000 books and 2000 manuscripts.

Matthias Fountain

Facing the Royal Palace's large courtyard to the northwest is the Romantic-style **Matthias Fountain** (Mátyás kút), portraying the young king Matthias Corvinus in hunting garb. To the right below him is Szép Ilona (Beautiful Helen). The middle one of the king's three dogs was blown up during the war; canine-loving Hungarians quickly had an exact copy made.

Statues & Monuments

Near the Habsburg Steps is a bronze statue from 1905 of the **Turul**, a totemic bird important in Magyar folklore. In front of Building C stands a statue of **Eugene of Savoy**, the Habsburg prince who wiped out the last Turkish army in Hungary at the Battle of Zenta in 1697. On the other side of the building is a **Hortobágyi csikós**, a Hungarian cowboy in full regalia.

Understand
Tivadar Kosztka Csontváry

Many critics consider Tivadar Kosztka Csontváry – a symbolist artist whose tragic life is sometimes compared to van Gogh's – Hungary's greatest painter. Csontváry produced his major works in just a few years starting in 1903 when he was 50. His first exhibition (Paris, 1907) met with praise, but critics panned his showing in Budapest the following year. He died penniless just after WWI. View works including *Ruins of the Greek Theatre at Taormina* (1905) and *Pilgrimage to the Cedars of Lebanon* (1907), on the 1st floor of the Hungarian National Gallery's Building C.

Danube River

Sights

Fishermen's Bastion   MONUMENT

1 Map p28, D5

The bastion, a neo-Gothic masquerade that looks medieval and offers some of the best views in Budapest, was built as a viewing platform in 1905 by Frigyes Schulek, the architect behind Matthias Church. Its name was taken from the medieval guild of fishermen responsible for defending this stretch of the castle wall. The seven gleaming white turrets represent the Magyar tribes that entered the Carpathian Basin in the late 9th century. (Halászbástya; I Szentháromság tér; adult/concession 800/400Ft; ⏱9am-8pm Mar–mid-Oct; 🚌16, 16A, 116)

Matthias Church   CHURCH

2 Map p28, D5

Parts of Matthias Church date back 500 years, notably the carvings above the southern entrance. But basically Matthias Church (so named because King Matthias Corvinus married Beatrix here in 1474) is a neo-Gothic confection designed by the architect Frigyes Schulek in 1896. (Mátyás templom; ☎1-355 5657; www.matyas-templom. hu; I Szentháromság tér 2; adult/concession 1500/1000Ft; ⏱9am-5pm Mon-Sat, 1-5pm Sun; 🚌16, 16A, 116)

Music History Museum   MUSEUM

3 Map p28, C4

Housed in an 18th-century palace with a lovely courtyard, this wonderful little museum traces the development of music in Hungary from the 18th century to the present day in a half-dozen exhibition rooms. There are rooms devoted to the work of Béla Bartók, Franz Liszt and Joseph Haydn, with lots of instruments and original scores and manuscripts. (Zenetörténeti Múzeum; ☎1-214 6770; www.zti.hu/museum; I Táncsics Mihály utca 7; adult/6-26yr 600/300Ft; ⏱10am-4pm Tue-Sun; 🚌16, 16A, 116)

Buda Castle Labyrinth   CAVE

4 Map p28, D6

This 1200m-long cave system, located some 16m under the Castle District, contains a motley collection of displays in its joined-up labyrinths encompassing 10 halls. Expect the history of Dracula, dry ice mist, and displays of figures from different operas, with music carrying eerily underground. It's all good fun and a relief from the heat on a hot summer's day – it's always 20°C down here. If you dare, step into the tunnel where you're confronted with complete darkness. (Budavári Labirintus; ☎1-212 0207; www.labirintusbudapest.hu; I Úri utca 9 & Lovas út 4/a; adult/under 12yr/senior & student 2000/600/1500Ft; ⏱10am-7pm; 🚌16, 16A, 116)

Matthias Fountain (p27)

Hospital in the Rock

MUSEUM

5 Map p28, C6

Part of the Castle Hill caves network, this subterranean hospital was used extensively during the WWII siege of Budapest and during the 1956 Uprising. It contains original medical equipment as well as some 200 wax figures and is visited on a guided one-hour tour, which includes a walk through a Cold War–era nuclear bunker and an eight-minute introductory video. (Sziklakórház; ☏06 70 701 0101; www.sziklakorhaz.eu; I Lovas út 4/c; adult/concession 4000/2000Ft; ⊙10am-8pm; ☐16, 16A, 116)

Király Baths

BATHHOUSE

6 Map p28, E2

The four pools for soaking here, with water temperatures of between 26°C and 40°C, are genuine Turkish baths erected in 1570. The largest has a wonderful sky-lit central dome (though the place is begging for a renovation); the other three are small. There's also a steam room and sauna. The Király is open to both men and women daily. (Király Gyógyfürdő; ☏1-202 3688; www.kiralyfurdo.hu; II Fő utca 84; daily tickets incl locker/cabin 2400/2700Ft; ⊙9am-9pm; ☐109, ☐4, 6, 19, 41)

Local Life

Self-Service Lunch

Locals working on Castle Hill avoid the tourists by eating at the self-service **Fortuna Önkiszolgáló** (Map p28, C5; Fortune Self-Service Restaurant; ☑1-375 2401; I Fortuna utca 4; mains 2200-4400Ft; ☺11.30am-2.30pm Mon-Fri; ▣16, 16A, 116). Cheap, cheerful and very convenient.

Eating

Budavári Rétesvár   HUNGARIAN €

 7 ✕ Map p28, C6

Strudel in all its permutations – from poppyseed with sour cherry to dill with cheese and cabbage – is available at this hole-in-the wall dispensary in a narrow alley of the Castle District. (Strudel Castle; ☑06 70 408 8696; www.budavariretesvar.hu; I Balta köz 4; strudel 310Ft; ☺8am-7pm; ▣16, 16A, 116)

Csalogány 26   INTERNATIONAL €€

8 ✕ Map p28, C3

Definitely one of the better restaurants in town, this intimate place with spartan decor turns its creativity to its superb food. Try the suckling *mangalica* (a kind of pork) with savoy cabbage (4900Ft) or other meat-heavy dishes that make the most of local ingredients. A three-course set lunch is a budget-pleasing 2900Ft. (☑1-201 7892; www.csalogany26.hu; I Csalogány utca 26; mains 3800-5300Ft; ☺noon-3pm & 7-10pm Tue-Sat; ▣11, 111)

Mandragóra   HUNGARIAN €€

9 ✕ Map p28, D2

With a hint of black magic in its name and a cosy location in the basement of a residential block, this family-run restaurant has earned loyal local fans with its excellent takes on Hungarian classics. Feast on slow-cooked duck with red cabbage, grey cattle sausage or pearl barley risotto. The weekly specials are a bargain. (☑1-202 2165; www.mandragorakavehaz.hu; II Kacsa utca 22; mains 2000-4200Ft; ☺11am-11pm Mon & Tue, to midnight Wed-Sat; ▣11, 111, ▣19, 41)

Zóna   INTERNATIONAL €€

10 ✕ Map p28, E7

Where the beautiful set eat and sup, Zóna is as much an architectural triumph as a foodie magnet. The menu is succinct and nicely executed; we particularly like the wild duck with vanilla-potato dumplings and the selection of Hungarian cheeses paired with pear ice cream. There are burgers, too, if all you want is a quick bite. (☑06 30 422 5981; www.zonabudapest.com; I Lánchíd utca 7-9; mains 3400-6800Ft; ☺noon-midnight Mon-Sat; ▣19, 41)

Baltazár Grill & Wine Bar   STEAK €€

11 ✕ Map p28, B4

Free-range chickens, ducks, Styrian pork and juicy rib eyes, Wagyu steaks and onglets sizzle on the charcoal grill at this excellent restaurant. Hungarian classics are also well represented, with several vegetarian dishes completing the picture. If you're not peckish, you can make your way to the atmospheric wine bar instead to sample tipples from the Carpathian Basin. (☏1-300 7050; www.baltazarbudapest. com; Ⅰ Országház utca 3; mains 2760-8960Ft; ☺noon-11pm; 🚌16, 16A, 116)

Pierrot INTERNATIONAL €€€

 12 🍴 Map p28, C4

This very stylish and long-established restaurant, housed in what was a bakery in the Middle Ages, specialises in dishes of the Austro-Hungarian Empire, revamped for the 21st century. Expect the likes of lamb tartare, quail stuffed with foie gras and mushrooms, and duck breast with caramelised apple. Presentation is faultless; eat in the vaulted dining room or in the garden. (☏1-375 6971; www.pierrot.hu; Ⅰ Fortuna utca 14; mains 3840-7640Ft; ☺11am-midnight; 🚌16, 16A, 116)

Drinking

Kávé Műhely COFFEE

 13 🍷 Map p28, E3

This tiny coffee shop is one of the best in the city. These guys roast their own beans, and their cakes and sandwiches are fantastic. Too hot for coffee? They've got craft beers and homemade lemonades, too. The attached gallery stages vibrant contemporary art exhibitions. (☏06 30 852 8517; www.facebook. com/kavemuhely; Ⅱ Fő utca 49; ☺7.30am-

🔍 Local Life
Going Up

A real 'insider's' way to get to and from Castle Hill is from Ⅰ Dózsa tér (bus 16 from Pest), where you'll find a **lift** (Map p28, E8; 200Ft; ☺6am-7pm Mon, to 7.30pm Tue-Sat, 9am-6.30pm Sun; 🚌16, 16A) that will whisk you up to the National Széchenyi Library, in the heart of Castle Hill. Glass cases in the hallway where the lift starts and ends are filled with archaeological finds from the Royal Palace.

6.30pm Mon-Fri, 9am-5pm Sat & Sun; Ⓜ M2 Batthyány tér, 🚌19, 41)

Lánchíd Söröző BAR

14 🍷 Map p28, E6

As its name implies, this pub near the Chain Bridge head has a wonderful retro Magyar feel to it, with old movie posters and advertisements on the walls and red-checked cloths on the tables. A proper local place with friendly service. (Chain Bridge Pub; ☏1-214 3144; www.lanchidsorozo.hu; Ⅰ Fő utca 4; ☺11am-midnight; 🚌16, 16A, 🚌19, 41)

Ruszwurm Cukrászda CAFE

15 🍷 Map p28, C5

This diminutive cafe dating from 1827 is the perfect place for coffee and cakes (420Ft to 750Ft) in the Castle District. In high season it's almost always impossible to get a seat. (☏1-375 5284; www. ruszwurm.hu; Ⅰ Szentháromság utca 7; ☺10am-7pm Mon-Fri, to 6pm Sat & Sun; 🚌16, 16A, 116)

Belga Söröző
BAR

16 Map p28, E5

Dark, wood-panelled, underground bar specialising in an extensive range of Belgian beers. There are only six on tap, but there's a much more inspiring bottled selection, as well as Belgian nibbles such as *moules marinière* (mussels in white wine) to keep hunger at bay. (Belgian Brasserie; ☑1-201 5082; www.belgasorozo.com/fooldal; II Bem rakpart 12; ☺noon-midnight; ⛴19, 41)

Oscar American Bar
BAR

17 Map p28, B3

The decor is cinema inspired (Hollywood memorabilia on the wood-panelled walls, leather directors' chairs) and the beautiful crowd often act like they're on camera. Not to worry: the potent cocktails (950Ft to 2250Ft) – from daiquiris and cosmopolitans to champagne cocktails and mojitos – go down a treat. There's music most nights. (☑06 20 214 2525; www.oscarbar.hu; I Ostrom utca 14; ☺5pm-2am Mon-Thu, to 4am Fri & Sat; Ⓜ M2 Széll Kálmán tér)

Entertainment

Budavár Cultural Centre
LIVE MUSIC

18 ⭐ Map p28, E6

This cultural centre just below Buda Castle has frequent programs for children and adults, including the excellent Sebő Klub és Táncház at 7pm on the second Saturday of every month and the Regejáró Misztrál Folk Music Club at the same time on the last Sunday. (Budavári Művelődési Háza; ☑1-201 0324; www.bem6.hu; Bem rakpart 6; programs 800-1000Ft; ⛴19, 41)

Shopping

Bortársaság
WINE

19 🔒 Map p28, B3

Once known as the Budapest Wine Society, this place has a dozen or so retail outlets in the capital with an exceptional selection of Hungarian wines. No one, but no one, knows Hungarian wines like these guys do. (☑1-289 9357; www.bortarsasag.hu; I Batthyány utca 59; ☺10am-9pm Mon-Sat, to 7pm Sun; Ⓜ M2 Széll Kálmán tér; ⛴4, 6)

Herend
CERAMICS

20 🔒 Map p28, C5

For both contemporary and traditional fine porcelain, there is no other place to go but Herend, Hungary's answer to Wedgwood. Among the most popular motifs produced by the company is the Victoria pattern of butterflies and wildflowers, designed for the British queen during the mid-19th century. (☑1-225 1051; www.herend.com; I Szentháromság utca 5; ☺10am-6pm Mon-Fri, to 4pm Sat & Sun Apr-Oct, closes 2pm Sat & Sun Nov-Mar); ⛴16, 16A, 116)

Understand

Wines of Hungary

Wine has been made in Hungary since at least the time of the Romans. It is very much a part of Hungarian culture, but only in recent years has it moved on from the local tipple you drank at Sunday lunch or the over-wrought and overpriced thimble of rarefied red sipped in a Budapest wine bar to the all-singin', all-dancin', all-embracin' obsession that it is today.

Wine Regions

Hungary is divided into seven major wine-growing regions, but we're most interested in a half-dozen of their subdivisions. It's all a matter of taste but the most distinctive and exciting Hungarian red wines come from Eger in the Northern Uplands and Villány in Southern Transdanubia. The best dry whites are produced around Lake Balaton's northern shore and in Somló, though the latest craze is for-dry, slightly tart *furmint* from Tokaj, which also makes the world-renowned sweet wine.

Buying & Choosing

Wine is sold by the glass or bottle everywhere and usually at reasonable prices. Old-fashioned wine bars ladle out plonk by the *deci* (decilitre; 0.1L), but if you're into more serious wine, you should visit one of Budapest's wine bars, such as DiVino Borbár (p83), Doblo (p103) or Kadarka (p97) wine restaurants like Borkonyha (p81) and Fióka (p57) or specialty wine shops like the Bortársaság (p34) chain.

When choosing a Hungarian wine, look for the words *minőségi bor* (quality wine) or *különleges minőségi bor* (premium quality wine). On a wine label the first word indicates the region, the second the grape variety (eg Villányi *kékfrankos*) or the type or brand of wine (eg Tokaji Aszú, Szekszárdi Bikavér). Other important words that you'll see include *édes* (sweet), *fehér* (white), *félédes* (semisweet), *félszáraz* (semidry or medium), *pezsgő* (sparkling), *száraz* (dry) and *vörös* (red).

Wine & Food Pairing

The pairing of food with wine is as great an obsession in Hungary as it is in France. Try a glass of Tokaji Aszú with savoury foods like foie gras or a strong cheese. A bone-dry *olaszrizling* goes well with fish; pork dishes are nice with a new *furmint* or any type of red, especially *kékfrankos*. Try *hárslevelű* with poultry.

Explore

Gellért Hill & Tabán

Gellért Hill (Gellért-hegy) is a 235m-high rocky hill southeast of
Castle Hill, crowned with a fortress (of sorts) and the spectacular
Liberty Monument, which has become Budapest's unofficial symbol.
You can't beat the views of the Royal Palace or the Danube and its
fine bridges from up here (as pictured). The leafy area below the
two hills is called Tabán.

The Sights in a Day

Start the day with a climb up Gellért Hill to explore the **Citadella** (p40), admire the lovely lady proclaiming peace throughout the land and ogle the vistas. Keep wandering and explore the impressive **Castle Garden Bazaar** (p44).

The **Aranyszarvas** (p45) is a relatively convenient place for lunch and an excellent choice in fine weather. Afterwards, depending on the day of the week and your sex, make your way to either the **Rudas Baths** (p44) or the **Gellért Baths** (p38) for a relaxing afternoon of soaking and/or swimming.

Wrap up your day with a beer or two at the **B8 Craft Beer & Pálinka Bar** (p45). Later in the evening walk towards the Danube and board the **A38** (p46). You may never come ashore again.

 Top Sights

Gellért Baths (p38)

Citadella & Liberty Monument (p40)

♥ **Best of Budapest**

Eating
Marcello (p44)

Thermal Baths & Pools
Gellért Baths (p38)

Rudas Baths (p44)

Getting There

🚌 **Bus** XI Szent Gellért tér can be reached from V Ferenciek tere in Pest on bus 7, and from points in Óbuda or south Buda on bus 86. Bus 27 runs almost to the top of Gellért Hill from XI Móricz Zsigmond körtér.

Ⓜ **Metro** The M4 metro line has stations at XI Gellért tér and XI Móricz Zsigmond körtér.

🚊 **Tram** XI Szent Gellért tér is linked to Déli station by tram 18, and to I Batthyány tér by tram 19. Trams 47 and 49 cross over to Pest and follow the Little Ring Rd from the same place. Trams 41 and 47 run south along XI Fehérvári út – useful for several entertainment venues in the area.

Top Sights
Gellért Baths

Soaking in the thermal waters of the art nouveau Gellért Baths, open to both men and women in mixed areas, is an awesome experience, and has been likened to taking a bath in a cathedral. The eight thermal pools range in temperature from 19°C to 38°C, and the water – high in calcium, magnesium and hydrogen carbonate – is said to be good for joint pains, arthritis and blood circulation.

Gellért gyógyfürdő

◉ Map p42, C4

www.gellertbath.hu

XI Kelenhegyi út 4, Danubius Hotel Gellért

⊙6am-8pm

🚌7, 86, Ⓜ️M4 Szent Gellért tér, 🚋18, 19, 47, 49

History

The springs here were favoured by the Turks as they were hotter than the others in Buda. In the 17th century the site was named Sárosfürdő (Mud Bath) after the fine silt that was pushed up with the spring water and settled at the bottom of the pools. The Gellért Baths as we know them today opened in 1918; they were expanded in 1927 by an outdoor wave bath and in 1934 by an indoor effervescent whirlpool.

In Hot Water

At the Gellért Baths (like most other baths nowadays) you are given an electronic bracelet that directs you to and then opens your locker or cabin. In the past it was a bit more complicated: you would find a free locker or cabin yourself and – after you got changed in (or beside) it – you would call the attendant, who would lock it for you and hand you a numbered tag. You had to remember your locker number; in a bid to prevent thefts the number on the tag was not the same as the one on the locker.

Swimming Pools

The swimming pools (included in the price) at the Gellért are mixed. The indoor ones, open year-round, are the most beautiful in Budapest; the outdoor wave pool (open May to September) has lovely landscaped gardens and 26ºC water.

☑ Top Tips

▶ Along with a bathing suit (which can be rented for 2000Ft), you might want to bring a pair of flip-flops (thongs), and a towel, as the sheets provided are not very absorbent.

▶ Everyone must use a bathing cap in the swimming pools; bring your own or use the disposable ones for 700Ft.

▶ Prices for the baths are: with locker/cabin Mon-Fri 5100/5500Ft, Sat & Sun 5300/5700Ft

---

✗ Take a Break

On trendifying XI Bartók Béla út, around the corner from the baths, you'll find several eating options.

Vegan Love (mains 1490-1590Ft; ⊙11am-8pm Mon-Sat, noon-8pm Sun; 🖉) serves oh-so-healthy and rather unusual vegan street food.

The Kelet Cafe & Gallery (p46), serves soups and salads along with the usual coffee and cakes.

Top Sights
Citadella & Liberty Monument

The Citadella atop Gellért Hill is a fortress that never saw battle. Built by the Habsburgs after the 1848–49 War of Independence to defend against further insurrection, by the time it was ready two years later the political climate had changed. To the southeast stands the Liberty Monument, the lovely lady with a palm frond in her outstretched arms proclaiming freedom.

Citadel

👁 Map p42, B3

🚌 27

admission free

Cave Church

Citadella

The Citadella is a U-shaped structure measuring 220m by 60m and built around a central courtyard. It was given to the city in the 1890s, and parts of it were symbolically blown to pieces. Today the fortress contains some big guns peeping through its loopholes, but the interior has been closed to the public while its future is decided.

Liberty Monument

Standing 14m high, the monument was erected in 1947 to honour the Soviet soldiers who died liberating Budapest in 1945. But the names of the fallen (once spelt out in Cyrillic letters on the plinth) and the statues of the soldiers themselves were removed in 1992, and sent to what is now called Memento Park (p48).

Cave Church

On the way up the hill on foot, have a peek at the **Cave Church**, built into a cave in 1926 and the seat of the Pauline order here until 1951, when the priests were arrested and imprisoned by the communists and the cave sealed off. It was reopened and reconsecrated in 1992. Behind it is a monastery with neo-Gothic turrets.

Liberty & Elizabeth Bridges

The spans below are Liberty Bridge to the south and Elizabeth Bridge to the north. The former, which opened in time for the Millenary Exhibition in 1896, has a fin-de-siècle cantilevered span. Gleaming white Elizabeth Bridge, dating from 1964, enjoys a special place in the hearts of many Budapesters as it was the first newly designed bridge to reopen after WWII, when the retreating Germans had destroyed all the bridges.

☑ Top Tips

▶ From the Citadella walk west for a few minutes along Citadella sétány to a lookout with one of the best vantage points in Budapest.

▶ To get to the Citadella on foot take the stairs leading up behind the St Gellért Monument or, from the Cave Church, follow XI Verejték utca (Perspiration St) through the park starting at the Cave Church.

▶ To avoid the steep climb, just hop on bus 27.

✖ Take a Break

For a proper sit-down meal, walk down the steps behind the St Gellért Monument and head north to Aranyszarvas (p45). It serves some excellent (and unusual) game dishes.

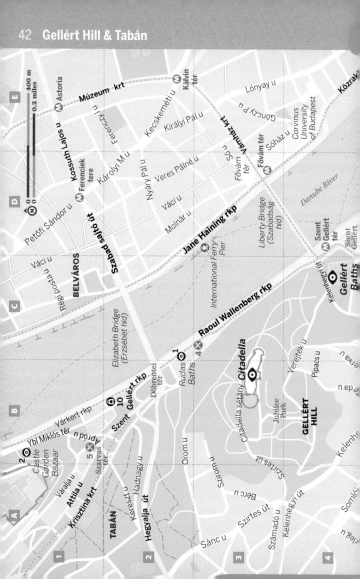

400 m
0.2 miles

E

Astoria Ⓜ
Múzeum krt
Kálvin tér Ⓜ
Lónyay u
Ferenc krt
Kecskeméti u
Királyi Pál u
Gönczy P u
Közr
Corvinus University of Budapest

D
Ⓜ
Ⓜ Ferenc u
Kossuth Lajos u
Ferenc n | Közp u
Ferenciek tere
Ferenc M u
Nyáry Pál u
Veres Pálné u
Sóház u
Fővám tér
Vámház krt
Só u
Fővám tér
Petőfi Sándor u
Károlyi M u
Váci u
Molnár u

C
Régi posta u
Váci u
BELVÁROS
Szabad sajtó út
Jane Haining rkp
International Ferry Pier
Danube River
Liberty Bridge (Szabadság híd)
Szent Gellért tér
Szent Gellért
Gellért Baths
Kelenhegyi út
Ⓜ

B
Ybl Miklós tér
Várkert rkp
Várkert Bazár
Castle Garden Bazaar
Elizabeth Bridge (Erzsébet híd)
Szent Gellért rkp
Döbrentei tér
Raoul Wallenberg rkp
Rudas Baths Ⓧ
Citadella
Citadella sétány
Vereték u
Pipacs u
erva u
Jubilee Park
GELLÉRT HILL
Kelenh

A
Ⓜ 2
Váralja u
Attila u
n pojdA
Szarvas tér
Hadnagy u
Erzsébet u
Keresztt u
Hegyalja út
Orom u
Sánc u
Szirom u
Berc u
Szirtes út
Számadó u
Szirtes út
Kelenhegyi út
Somlói
Somlói
TABÁN
Krisztina krt

🅐 10
🅐 5

1
2
3
4

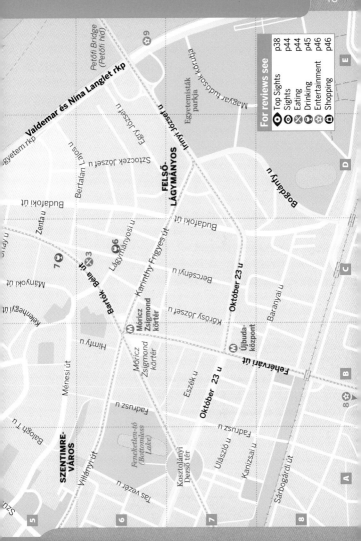

Petőfi Bridge
(Petőfi híd)

⭐ 9

Egyetemisták
parkja

Magyar tudósok körútja

Valdemar és Nina Langlet rkp

gyetem rkp

Budafoki út

Zenta u

FELSŐ-
LÁGYMÁNYOS

Sztoczek József u

Egry József u

Bertalan Lajos u

Bogdány u

Budafoki út

Irinyi József u

n Apjo

Manyoki út

Kelenhegyi út

Bartók Béla út

Lágymányosi u

Karinthy Frigyes út

Bercsényi u

Oktober 23 u

Baranyai u

7 ⭐

6 ⭐
3 ⭐

Móricz
Zsigmond
körtér

Kőrösy József u

Ⓜ Újbuda-
központ

Himfy u

Móricz
Zsigmond
körtér

Ⓜ

Fehérvári út

Ménesi út

Eszék u

Oktober 23 u

Balogh T u

SZENTIMRE-
VÁROS

Villányi út

Tas vezér u

Fadrusz u

Fenéketlen-tó
(Bottomless
Lake)

Kosztolányi
Dezső tér

Ulászló u

Fadrusz u

Kanizsai u

Sárbogárdi út

8 ⭐

Szü

For reviews see	
◉ Top Sights	p38
◉ Sights	p44
✪ Eating	p44
✪ Drinking	p45
◉ Entertainment	p46
◉ Shopping	p46

Sights

Rudas Baths
BATHHOUSE

1 ⊙ Map p42, C2

Built in 1566, these renovated baths are the most Turkish in Budapest, with an octagonal pool, domed cupola with coloured glass and massive columns. It's a real zoo on mixed weekend nights, when bathing costumes (rental 1300Ft) are compulsory. You can enter the lovely **swimming pool** (I Döbrentei tér 9; with locker Mon-Fri/Sat & Sun 2900/3200Ft, with thermal bath 3800/4200Ft; ⊙6am-8pm daily, plus 10pm-4am Fri & Sat) separately if you're more interested in swimming than soaking. (Rudas Gyógyfürdő; ☑1-356 1322; www.rudasfurdo.hu; I Döbrentei tér 9; with cabin Mon-Fri/Sat & Sun 3200/3500Ft, morning/night ticket 2500/4600Ft; ⊙men 6am-8pm Mon & Wed-Fri, women 6am-8pm Tue, mixed 10pm-4am Fri, 6am-8pm & 10pm-4am Sat, 6am-8pm Sun; ☐7, 86, ☐18, 19)

Castle Garden Bazaar
HISTORIC SITE

2 ⊙ Map p42, B1

The reopening of this renovated pleasure park (dating from 1893) has added a whole new dimension to Tabán. The complex comprises over a dozen neo-Gothic and neo-Renaissance structures including a theatre, convention centre and, in the Southern Palaces, a large gallery with cutting-edge exhibitions. A staircase and lift from Lánchíd utca leads to the Neo-Renaissance Garden and stairs, lifts and an escalator take you up to Castle Hill. The huge Foundry Courtyard boasts a restaurant with terrace and large performance space. (Várkert Bazár; ☑1-225 0554; www.varkertbazar.hu; Ybl Miklós tér 6; ☐86, ☐19, 41)

Eating

Marcello
ITALIAN €

3 ✕ Map p42, C6

A perennial favourite with students from the nearby university since it opened more than a quarter-century ago, this family-owned operation just down the road from XI Szent Gellért tér offers reliable Italian fare at affordable prices. The pizzas (1280Ft to 1900Ft) and the salad bar are good value, as is the lasagne (1600Ft), which is legendary in these parts. (☑06 30 243 5229, 1-466 6231; www.marcelloetterem.hu; XI Bartók Béla út 40; mains 1500-4000Ft; ⊙noon-10pm Sun-Wed, to 11pm Thu-Sat; ☐6)

Rudas Restaurant & Bar
INTERNATIONAL €€

4 ✕ Map p42, C3

We love, love, love this place with its turquoise interior and stunning views of the Danube and bridges. It sits above the Rudas Baths Wellness Centre (ask about inclusive packages) so it's just the ticket after a relaxing massage or treatment. The smallish outside terrace is a delight in summer (though it can be

Rudas Baths

noisy). (📞06 20 921 4877; www.rudarest aurant.hu; Döbrentei tér 9, Rudas Baths; mains 2450-4350Ft; 🕐11am-10pm; 🚌7, 86, 🚋18, 19)

Aranyszarvas
HUNGARIAN €€

5 🍴 Map p42, B1

Set in an 18th-century inn literally down the steps from the southern end of Castle Hill (views!), the 'Golden Stag' serves up some very meaty and unusual dishes (try the venison in fruity game sauce, the saddle of boar with dried tomatoes or the duck breast with Savoy cabbage). The covered outside terrace is a delight in summer. (📞1-375 6451; www.aranyszarvas.hu; I Szarvas tér 1; mains 2750-3600Ft; 🕐noon-11pm Tue-Sat; 🚌86, 🚋18)

Drinking

B8 Craft Beer & Pálinka Bar
CRAFT BEER

6 🍺 Map p42, C6

Our favourite new watering hole in Buda has more than two-dozen craft beers available from Hungary's 52 (at last count) breweries. Look for the names Legenda, Monyo and Etyeki and try the last's Belga Búza (Belgian Wheat). Harder stuff? Some 10 types of *pálinka* (fruit brandy) – from Japanese plum to Gypsy cherry. (B8 Kézműves Sör és Pálinkabár; 📞1-791 3462; www.facebook.com/b8pub; Bercsényi utca 8; 🕐4-11pm Mon, noon-11pm Tue-Fri, 5-11pm Sat; Ⓜ M4 Móricz Zsigmond körtér, 🚌18, 19, 47, 49)

Q Local Life

Drinking Cure

If you don't like getting wet or you don't have the time for a thermal bath, do what locals do and try a 'drinking cure' by visiting the **Pump Room** (Map p42, B2; Ivócsarnok; I Erzsébet híd; ⊙11am-6pm Mon, Wed & Fri, 7am-2pm Tue & Thu; ⑤86, ⑤19, 41), just below the western end of Elizabeth Bridge. A half-litre/litre of the hot, smelly water – meant to cure whatever ails you – is just 50/80Ft. Bring your own container.

Kelet Cafe & Gallery   CAFE

7 Map p42, C5

This really cool cafe moonlights as a used-book exchange on the ground floor and a large, bright gallery with seating upstairs. There are foreign newspapers to read and soups (780Ft to 990Ft) and sandwiches (850Ft to 1100Ft) should you feel peckish. Try the super hot chocolate. (Kelet Kávézó és Galéria; ☎06 20 230 0094; www.facebook.com/keletkavezo; Bartók Béla út 29; ⊙7.30am-11pm Mon-Fri, 9am-11pm Sat & Sun; ⓂM4 Móricz Zsigmond körtér, ⑤18, 19, 47, 49)

Entertainment

Fonó Buda Music House   LIVE MUSIC

8 ⭐ Map p42, B8

This venue has *táncház* (folk music and dance) programs several times a week (especially on Wednesday) at 6.30pm or 8pm, as well as concerts by big-name bands (mostly playing world music) throughout the month; it's one of the best venues in town for this sort of thing. Consult the website for more details. (Fonó Budaio Zeneház; ☎1-206 5300; www.fono.hu; XI Sztregova utca 3; ⊙box office 9am-5pm Mon-Fri; ⑤41, 56)

A38   LIVE MUSIC

9 ⭐ Map p42, E6

Moored on the Buda side just south of Petőfi Bridge, the 'A38 Ship' is a decommissioned Ukrainian stone hauler from 1968 that has been recycled as a major live-music venue. It's so cool that Lonely Planet readers once voted it the best bar in the world. The ship's hold rocks throughout the year. Terraces open in the warmer weather. (☎1-464 3940; www.a38.hu; XI Pázmány Péter sétány 3-11; ⊙11am-midnight Sun-Thu, to 3am Fri & Sat; ⑤212, ⑤4, 6)

Shopping

Prezent   DESIGN

10 🔒 Map p42, B2

This shop specialising in 'sustainable Hungarian design' sells fashion and accessories as well as natural cosmetics. Earnest and admirable, and good stuff too! (www.prezentshop.hu; Döbrentei utca 16; ⊙10.30am-6pm Wed-Mon; ⑤18, 19, 41)

Understand

Raoul Wallenberg, Hero for All Times

The former Swedish Embassy on Gellért Hill bears a plaque attesting to the heroism of Raoul Wallenberg (1912–47), a Swedish diplomat and businessman who, together with his colleagues Carl-Ivan Danielsson (1880–1963) and Per Anger (1913–2002), rescued as many as 35,000 Hungarian Jews during WWII.

Wallenberg began working in 1936 for a trading firm whose owner was a Hungarian Jew. In July 1944, the Swedish Foreign Ministry, at the request of Jewish and refugee organisations in the USA, sent the 32-year-old Swede on a rescue mission to Budapest as an attaché to their embassy there. By that time almost half a million Jews in Hungary had been sent to Nazi death camps in Germany and Poland.

Rescue Mission

Wallenberg immediately began issuing Swedish safe-conduct passes (called 'Wallenberg passports') from the Swedish embassy in Budapest. He also set up a series of 'safe houses' (mostly in Újlipótváros and now marked with plaques) flying the flag of Sweden and other neutral countries where Jews could seek asylum. He even followed German 'death marches' and deportation trains, distributing food and clothing and actually pulling some 500 people off the cars along the way.

When the Soviet army entered Budapest in January 1945, Wallenberg went to report to the authorities but in the wartime confusion was arrested for espionage and sent to Moscow. In the early 1950s, responding to reports that Wallenberg had been seen alive in a labour camp, the Soviet Union announced that he had in fact died of a heart attack two years after the war ended. Many believe Wallenberg was executed by the Soviets, who suspected him of spying for the USA.

Lifetime Legacy

Wallenberg was made an honorary citizen of the city of Budapest in 2003. Other foreigners associated with helping Hungarian Jews in Budapest include Carl Lutz (1885–1975), a Swiss consul who has a memorial devoted to him on VII Dob utca in Pest, and Jane Haining (1897–1944), a Budapest-based Scottish missionary who died in Auschwitz. In 2010 the city of Budapest named sections of Danube river banks in their honour.

Top Sights
Memento Park

Getting There

Ⓜ M4 metro to Kelen-föld train station and then bus 101 or 150 (25 minutes, every 20 to 30 minutes).

🚌 The direct park bus departs from opposite the Ritz-Carlton Hotel on V Erzsébet tér.

Home to more than 40 statues, busts and plaques of Lenin, Marx, Béla Kun and others whose like-nesses have ended up on trash heaps elsewhere, Memento Park, 10km southwest of the city centre, is truly a mind-blowing place to visit. Ogle the socialist realism and try to imagine that some of these relics were erected as recently as the late 1980s.

Old Soviet style statue, Memento Park

The Monuments

Ogle the socialist realism and try to imagine that at least four of these monstrous relics were erected as recently as the late 1980s; a few of them, including the Béla Kun memorial of 'our hero' in a crowd by fence-sitting sculptor Imre Varga, were still in place as late as 1992.

Old Barracks Exhibition

An exhibition centre in an old barracks – Hungary was called 'the happiest barracks in the camp' under communism – has displays on the events of 1956 and the changes since 1989, as well as documentary film with rare footage of secret agents collecting information on 'subversives'. The Communist Hotline allows you to listen in on the likes of Lenin, Stalin and even Che Guevara.

Stalin's Boots

Excellent selfie ops include the reproduced remains of Stalin's boots (left after a crowd pulled the statue down from its plinth on XIV Dózsa György út during the 1956 Uprising) and an original two-stroke Trabant 601, the 'people's car' produced in East Germany.

The Shop

The museum gift shop is a treasure trove of kitsch communist memorabilia: pins, CDs of revolutionary songs, books and posters.

☎ 1-424 7500

www.mementopark.hu

XXII Balatoni út

adult/student 1500/1000Ft

🕙 10am-dusk

☑ Top Tips

▸ Book tickets online the day before and get a 40% discount.

▸ If you go via public transport the park website offers a Memento Park Bonus Tour of sights to follow along the way, including vintage *sörözők* (pubs), a military cemetery with the graves of American soldiers killed in Hungary during WWII and a plethora of Soviet-style apartment blocks.

✕ Take a Break

Catering facilities are nonexistent at the park. Before you set out take a picnic or eat at one of the places in south Buda near the M4, such as the **Tranzit Art Café** (☎ 1-209 3070; www. tranzitcafe.com; XI Bukarest utca & Ulászló utca; 🕙 9am-11pm Mon-Fri, 10am-10pm Sat).

Explore

Óbuda

Óbuda is the oldest part of Buda and retains a lost-in-the-past village feel. The narrow streets hide excellent museums and legendary eateries, while the remains of the Roman settlement of Aquincum lie further north. The Buda Hills offer great walking, the loftiest views of the city and forms of transport that will delight all kids. Adventurers can explore under the city by venturing into the three accessible caves.

The Sights in a Day

☼ Start the day with a wake-up splash at the **Veli Bej Baths** (p54) and then fritter the morning away jumping in and out of the various pools and just relaxing. If you feel up to it, climb the hill a short distance to the west to view **Gül Baba's Tomb** (p54). It's a unique sight in this part of Europe.

☀ For coffee, stop at nearby **Barako Kávéház** (p57). Next, take a closer look at fin-de-siècle Óbuda – both the **Vasarely Museum** (p54) and the **Hungarian Museum of Trade & Tourism** (p55) deserve your attention.

☽ Check to see what's playing at the **Óbuda Society** (p57) and plan your evening accordingly. **Kéhli Vendéglő** (p57) is just next door – convenient if you want to eat before or just after the performance. Otherwise head to **Fuji Japán** (p57) for some of the city's finest Japanese cuisine.

 Best of Budapest

Eating
Kéhli Vendéglő (p57)

Fióka (p57)

Fuji Japán (p57)

Museums & Galleries
Vasarely Museum (p54)

Hungarian Museum of Trade & Tourism (p55)

Getting There

🚌 **Bus** Bus 109 runs north from II Batthyány tér through much of Óbuda; bus 9 follows largely the same route. Buses 34 and 106 link Aquincum to III Szentlélek tér in Óbuda. Bus 291 links the chairlift's lower terminus on XII Zugligeti út with II Szilágyi Erzsébet fasor.

🚋 **Tram** Trams 1 and 1A run along XIII Róbert Károly körút from City Park in Pest to Árpád Bridge in Óbuda. Trams 59 and 61 connect II Széll Kálmán tér with the Cog Railway's lower terminus. Trams 17, 19 and 41 link III Bécsi út with II Margit körút and Gellért Hill, respectively.

🚃 **HÉV** Szentlélek tér and Tímár utca stops serve Óbuda; the Aquincum stop is handy for the Roman ruins.

ÓBUDA

Imre Varga 6
Collection

Fő tér

Szentlélek
tér

Vasarely 1
Museum

Szentlélek tér

Serfőző u

Tél u

5 Hungarian Museum
of Trade & Tourism

Timár u

Lajos u

10
14

Kis Korona u

Perc u

P

Textilgyár u

Flórián
tér

Kiscelli u

Pacsirtamező u

Dévai
Bíró M
tér

Lajos u

Szőlő u

Beszterce u

Viador u

Bokor u

6

ÚJLAK

Reménység u

Föld u

Zápor u

Kenyeres u

Selmeci u

Hungarian Federation
of Disabled Persons'
Associations

San Marco u

Bécsi út

Tégla u

Doberdó út

Kiscelli u

Kiscell 2
Museum

Kolostor út

MÁTYÁSHEGY

Folyondár u

Szépvölgyi út

REMETEHEGY

400 m
0.2 miles

Remetehegyi út

Mátyás-
hegy

Mátyáshegyi út

Virág Benedek u

Felső Zöldmáli út

Remete köz

Nyereg út

7

12

8

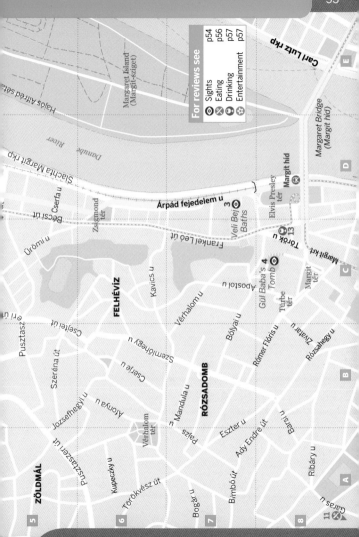

For reviews see

⊙ Sights	p54
✕ Eating	p56
🍷 Drinking	p57
☆ Entertainment	p57

Sights

Vasarely Museum
GALLERY

1 Map p52, E1

Installed in the imposing Zichy Mansion (Zichy kastély), built in 1757, this museum contains the works of Victor Vasarely (or Vásárhelyi Győző, as he was known before he emigrated to Paris in 1930), the late 'father of op art'. The works, especially *Keek* and *Ibadan-Pos,* are excellent and fun to watch as they 'swell' and 'move' around the canvas. Closed for renovation until late 2017. (☑1-388 7551; www.vasarely.hu; III Szentlélek tér 6; adult/6-26yr 800/400Ft; ☉10am-5.30pm Tue-Sun; 🚊29, 109, 🚇Szentlélek tér)

Kiscell Museum
MUSEUM

2 Map p52, B2

Housed in an 18th-century monastery, this museum contains three excellent sections. Downstairs you'll find a complete 19th-century apothecary brought from Kálvin tér; a wonderful assembly of ancient signboards advertising shops and other trades; and rooms dressed in empire, Biedermeier and art nouveau furniture. An impressive collection of works by contemporary artists József Rippl-Rónai, Lajos Tihanyi, István Csók and Béla Czóbel is upstairs. The juxtaposition of the stark Gothic church shell against the temporary multimedia and art exhibits is visually arresting. (Kiscelli Múzeum; ☑1-250 0304; www.kiscellimuzeum.hu; III Kiscelli utca 108; adult/ concession 1600/800Ft; ☉10am-6pm Tue-Sun Apr-Oct, to 4pm Tue-Sun Nov-Mar; 🚊29, 109, 🚇17, 19, 41)

Veli Bej Baths
BATHHOUSE

3 Map p52, D7

One of the oldest (1575) and most beautiful Ottoman-era baths in Budapest, with five thermal pools of varying temperatures – the central pool lies under a beautiful cupola. The water is high in sodium, potassium and calcium and good for joint ailments, chronic arthritis and calcium deficiency. There's also a cluster of saunas and steam rooms; massage available. (Veli Bej Fürdője; ☑1-438 8500; www.irgalmas.hu/veli-bej-furdo; II Árpád fejedelem útja 7 & Frankel Leó út 54; 6am-noon 2240Ft, 3-7pm 2800Ft, after 7pm 2000Ft; ☉6am-noon & 3-9pm; 🚊9, 109, 🚇4, 6, 17, 19)

Gül Baba's Tomb
ISLAMIC TOMB

4 Map p52, C8

This reconstructed tomb contains the mortal remains of Gül Baba, an Ottoman dervish who took part in the capture of Buda in 1541 and is known in Hungary as the 'Father of Roses'. The tomb and mosque are a pilgrimage place for Muslims, especially from Turkey, and you must remove your shoes before entering. From Török utca, walk up steep Gül Baba utca to the set of steps just past No 16. Closed for renovation at research time. (Gül Baba türbéje; ☑1-237 4400; www.museum.hu/budapest/gulbabaturbe; II Türbe tér 1; admission free; ☉10am-6pm; 🚇4, 6, 17)

Gül Baba's Tomb

Hungarian Museum of Trade & Tourism
MUSEUM

5 Map p52, E2

This excellent little museum traces Budapest's catering and hospitality trade through the ages, including the dramatic changes post-WWII, with restaurant items, tableware, advertising posters, packaging and original shop signs. Go upstairs for an intimate look at the lives of various tradespeople – from bakers and publicans to launderers. The lovely cafe is lit by antique lamps. A gem. (Magyar Kereskedelmi és Vendéglátó-ipari Múzeum; ☑1-375 6249; www.mkvm.hu; III Korona tér 1; adult/student 1000/500Ft; ☺10am-6pm Tue-Sun; ☒29, 109, ☒Tímár utca)

Imre Varga Collection
GALLERY

6 Map p52, E1

This collection includes sculptures, statues, medals and drawings by Imre Varga (b 1923), one of Hungary's foremost sculptors. Like others before him, notably Zsigmond Kisfaludi Strobl, Varga seems to have sat on both sides of the fence politically for decades – sculpting Béla Kun and Lenin as dexterously as he did St Stephen, Béla Bartók and even Imre Nagy. But his work always remains fresh and is never derivative. Note the fine bust of Winston Churchill (2003) near the entrance. (Varga Imre Gyűjtemény; ☑1-250 0274; www.budapest galeria.hu; III Laktanya utca 7; adult/student

Top Tip

Béla Bartók Memorial House

Visit the great composer's house (Map p52, A3, Bartók Béla Emlékház; 📞1-394 2100; www.bartokmuseum.hu; II Csalán út 29; 1500Ft; ⏰10am-5pm Tue-Sun; 🚌5, 29, 🚋61) for 'free' by attending one of the regularly scheduled concerts there. You'll see the old Edison recorder (complete with wax cylinders) that Bartók used to record Hungarian folk music in Transylvania, as well as his beloved hand-carved dining-room furniture, and even half a cigarette he smoked!

& senior 800/400Ft; ⏰10am-6pm Tue-Sun Apr-Oct, to 4pm Tue-Sun Nov-Mar; 🚌29, 109, 🚋Szentlélek tér)

Pálvölgy Cave   CAVE

 7 ⓞ Map p52, A3

The second-largest in Hungary, this 29km-long cave discovered in 1904 is noted for both its spectacular stalactites and rock formations. Tours last 45 minutes and depart at 10.15am (last tour at 4.15pm) from the lowest level, taking you through dank, claustrophobia-inducing passages and up several hundred steps. Highlights include John's Lookout in the largest of chambers, as well as Radium Hall, reminiscent of Dante's Inferno. The temperature is a constant 11°C so wear a jacket or jumper. (Pálvölgyi-barlang; 📞1-325 9505; www.palvolgyi.atw.

hu; II Szépvölgyi út 162/a; adult/concession 1400/1100Ft, joint ticket with Szemlőhegy Cave 2000/1600Ft; ⏰10am-5pm Tue-Sun; 🚌65)

Eating

Náncsi Néni   HUNGARIAN €€

8 ✕ Map p52, A4

Auntie Náncsi (Hungarian for any loopy old lady) is a favourite with locals and expats alike, and she's very much of sound mind. Located up in Hűvösvölgy, this restaurant specialises in game in autumn and winter, plus goose liver dishes. In summer it's the lighter fare – lots of stuff cooked with grapes and morello cherries – and garden seating that attracts. (Auntie Nancy; 📞1-397 2742; www.nancsineni.hu; II Ördögárok út 80; mains 850-3450Ft; ⏰noon-11pm Mon-Fri, 9am-11pm Sat & Sun; 🚌63, 157)

Sushi Sei   JAPANESE €€

9 ✕ Map p52, D4

This stylish restaurant is one of the best spots in Budapest for a wide spectrum of authentic Japanese cuisine. Apart from beautifully presented nigiri, sushi and tempura sets, you can feast on cold soba noodles, yakitori, tonkatsu and grilled fish. The bento boxes (1900Ft to 2200Ft) are particularly good value. (📞1-240 4065; www.sushisei.hu; III Bécsi út 58; mains 2000-6300Ft; ⏰noon-10pm Sun-Thu, to 11pm Fri & Sat; 🚌17, 19, 41)

Kéhli Vendéglő HUNGARIAN €€

10 Map p52, E2

Self-consciously rustic, Kéhli has some of the best traditional Hungarian food in town. One of Hungary's best-loved writers, the novelist Gyula Krúdy (1878–1933), who lived in nearby Dugovics Titusz tér, moonlighted as a restaurant critic and enjoyed Kéhli's *forró velőscsont fokhagymás pirítós-sal* (bone marrow on toast; 980Ft) so much that he included it in one of his novels. (☑1-368 0613; www.kehli.hu; III Mókus utca 22; mains 1490-6990Ft; ☉noon-midnight; ☐29, 109, ☐Szentlélek tér, Tímár utca)

Fióka HUNGARIAN €€

11 Map p52, A8

This light, bright bistro and wine bar has a succinct, imaginative menu, featuring such treats as smoked goose carpaccio and bone marrow on toast. The great selection of wines is not just from Hungary but the whole Carpathian Basin, and there's a supporting cast of *pálinkas* (fruit brandies). (☑1-426 5555; www.facebook.com/fiokavarosmajor; XII Városmajor utca 75; mains 2460-5900Ft; ☉11am-midnight Wed-Sun; ☐56, 59, 61)

Fuji Japán JAPANESE €€€

12 Map p52, A4

It's well worth travelling into the hills of posh district II for the most authentic Japanese food in town. Apart from super-fresh sashimi sets and imaginative sushi rolls, repeat clients

come for hotpots, yakitori and more. For a special occasion, opt for tatami seating and blow your budget on a 10-course *kaiseki* menu (18,500Ft). Set weekday lunch is just 2290Ft. (☑1-325 7111; www.fujirestaurant.hu; II Csatárka út 54; mains 2800-11,900Ft; ☉noon-11pm; ☐29)

Drinking

Barako Kávéház COFFEE

13 Map p52, C8

Run by a tattooed Filipino, this thimble-sized coffee house aims to spread the fame of Liberica Baraco coffee from the Philippines. While arabica tastes sour when cold, Liberica Baraco retains its sweetness. In addition to latte, ristretto and other standards, you can also fortify yourself with ice drip Dutch coffee here. (☑06 30 283 7065; www.barakokavehaz.com; II Török utca 3; ☉8am-8pm Mon-Sat, 9am-6pm Sun; ☐4, 6, 19, 41)

Entertainment

Óbuda Society CONCERT VENUE

14 Map p52, D2

This very intimate venue in Óbuda takes its music seriously and hosts recitals and some chamber orchestras. Highly recommended. (Óbudai Társaskör; ☑1-250 0288; www.obudaitarsaskor.hu; III Kis Korona utca 7; tickets 1000-4500Ft; ☐86, ☐Tímár utca)

Top Sights
Aquincum

Getting There

🚋 HÉV to Aquincum

🚌 34, 106

Aquincum, dating from the end of the 1st century AD and the most complete Roman civilian town in Hungary, had paved streets and sumptuous single-storey houses, complete with courtyards, fountains and mosaic floors, as well as sophisticated drainage and heating systems. It's not all immediately apparent as you explore the ruins in the open-air archaeological park, but the museum puts it in perspective.

Aquincum Museum

The museum, next to the entrance to the Roman town, contains an impressive collection of household objects – pottery, weaponry, grooming implements, a military discharge diploma... In the basement there are some hokey virtual games for kids, such as battling with a gladiator. Look out for the replica of a 3rd-century portable organ called a hydra, the mock-up of a Roman bath and a road map of the Roman Empire (*Tabula Peutingeriana*).

Painter's House & Mithraeum

Opposite the museum is the wonderful Painter's House, a re-created, furnished Roman dwelling from the 3rd century AD. Behind it is the Mithraeum, a temple dedicated to the god Mithra, the chief deity of a religion that once rivalled Christianity.

Main Thoroughfare

Just north of the museum, the arrow-straight main thoroughfare leads you past ruins of the large public baths, the *macellum* (market) and the *basilica* (court house). Most of the large stone sculptures and sarcophagi are in the old museum building to the east.

Roman Civilian Amphitheatre

Across III Szentendrei út to the northwest and close to the HÉV stop is the Roman Civilian Amphitheatre (Római polgári amfiteátrum; Zsófia utca & Szentendrei ut; admission free), about half the size of the amphitheatre reserved for the garrisons in Óbuda and seating 3000. Lions were kept in the small cubicles, while slain gladiators were carried through the 'Gate of Death' to the west.

---

www.aquincum.hu

III Szentendrei út 133-135

adult/concession museum & park 1600/800Ft, archaeological park only 1000/500Ft

⊙museum 10am-6pm Tue-Sun Apr-Oct, to 4pm Nov-Mar, park 9am-6pm Tue-Sun Apr-Oct

☑ Top Tips

▶ If travelling to Aquincum on the HÉV suburban train, view the Roman Civilian Amphitheatre first before crossing busy III Szentendrei út.

▶ Be aware tickets are almost always checked by HÉV conductors.

▶ If you bought a Castle Museum or Kiscell Museum ticket, it is valid for entry to the Aquincum Museum for 30 days.

✗ Take a Break

A branch of the popular **Nagyi Palacsintázója** (http://nagyipali.hu; III Szentendrei út 13; pancakes 190-680Ft; ⊙24hr; ✍) pancake chain is at the entrance to the Aquincum Museum.

Local Life
Touring the Buda Hills

Getting There

M Széll Kálmán tér metro station (M2).

🚌 59 or 61 to the Cog Railway lower terminus.

🚌 291 from the Chairlift terminus to II Szilágyi Erzsébet fasor

Visitors to Budapest head for the hills – the city's 'green lungs' – for a variety of reasons. There's great hiking, a couple of trip-worthy sights and the summer homes of well-heeled Budapest families to ogle. But locals come just to ride the unusual forms of transport on offer. It really can be said that getting to/from the Buda Hills is half the fun.

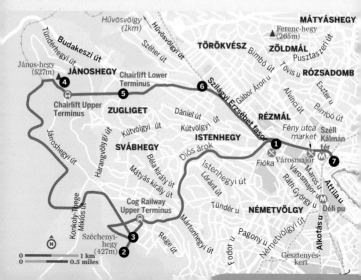

❶ Cog Railway Up

From Széll Kálmán tér metro station walk west along Szilágyi Erzsébet fasor for 10 minutes (or take tram 59 or 61 for two stops) to the lower terminus of the **Cog Railway** (Fogaskerekű vasút; www.bkv.hu; XII Szilágyi Erzsébet fasor 14-16; admission 1 BKV ticket or 350Ft; ⏱5am-11pm) just opposite the circular Hotel Budapest at No 47. Built in 1874, the railway climbs for 3.7km in 15 minutes three or four times an hour to Széchenyi-hegy (427m). On your way to the lower terminus, buy food supplies at **Fény utca market** (II Fény utca; ⏱6am-6pm Mon-Fri, to 2pm Sat) next to the Mammut shopping mall in II Széll Kálmán tér

❷ Picnic on Széchenyi-hegy

Here you can stop for your picnic in the attractive park south of the old-time railway station.

❸ Children's Railway

Just south on Hegyhát út opposite Rege út is the narrow-gauge **Children's Railway** (Gyermekvasút; ☎1-397 5394; www.gyermekvasut.hu; adult/child 1 section 600/300Ft, entire line 700/350Ft; ⏱closed Mon Sep-Apr). It was built in 1951 by Pioneers (socialist Scouts) and is now staffed entirely by schoolchildren aged 10 to 14 (the engineer excluded), the lovely little train chugs along for 11km, terminating at Hűvösvölgy 45 minutes later.

❹ Elizabeth Lookout

Trails fan out from any of the eight stops along the railway line or you can return to Széll Kálmán tér on tram 61 from Hűvösvölgy. Better still, disembark at János-hegy, the fourth stop and the highest point (527m) in the hills. From atop the 23.5m-tall **Elizabeth Lookout** (Erzsébet kilátó; Erzsébet kilátó utca; ⏱8am-8pm), with 134 steps, you can see the Tatra Mountains in Slovakia.

❺ Going Down

About 700m to the east of the tower is the **Chairlift** (Libegő; www.bkv.hu; 1 way/return adult 1000/1400Ft, 6-26yr 600/800Ft; ⏱10am-7pm May-Aug), which will take you 1040m down at 4km/h to XII Zugligeti út. From here bus 291 will take you to II Szilágyi Erzsébet fasor.

❻ Dinner in the Hills

The 291 stops right in front of **Szép Ilona** (☎1-275 1392; www.szepilona vendeglo.hu; II Budakeszi út 1-3; mains 1800-4500Ft; ⏱noon-11pm), a recently spruced-up Buda Hills spot that is the place to come for hearty indigenous fare. But if you'd like something a bit more, well, 21st century, **Fióka** (p57), a newish bistro and wine bar, is almost next to the Cog Railway's lower terminus.

❼ Nightcap

Stop for a drink or two at **Oscar American Bar** (p34) just up from II Széll Kálmán tér on the way to Castle Hill.

Explore

Belváros

The 'Inner Town' is just that – the centre of Pest's universe, especially when it comes to tourism. It's where you'll find Váci utca, with its luxury shops, restaurants and bars, and Vörösmarty tér, home to the city's most celebrated *cukrászda* (cake shop) and one of its three Michelin-starred restaurants. Belváros is the most heavily visited part of town boasting splendid art nouveau architecture and dining venues.

The Sights in a Day

☀️ Spend the morning strolling along **Váci utca** (p64) as far as **Vörösmarty tér** (p65), taking in the sights and perhaps doing a spot of shopping. For a view of Belváros like no other, hop on a BKV passenger ferry for a brief cruise along the river.

☼ If the weather's right, have lunch on the terrace at **Monk's Bistrot** (p68). Then head for **Pesti Vigadó** (p68); the expansive views of the river from its terrace are sensational.

☾ Round off the day with a coffee at **Gerbeaud** (p65) or a local brew from newcomer **Marionett Craft Beer House** (p70). For dinner with music you couldn't do better than **Kárpátia** (p68). Toward the bewitching hour, head north for V Erzsébet tér and the **Akvárium Klub** (p70). There's no hurry, though; the place raves till well past the break of day.

For a local's day in Belváros, see p64.

🔍 Local Life

Exploring Váci utca & Vörösmarty tér (p64)

❤️ Best of Budapest

Eating
Baraka (p69)

Monk's Bistrot (p68)

Kárpátia (p68)

Drinking
Centrál Kávéház (p70)

Gerbeaud (p65)

Shopping
Le Parfum Croisette (p71)

Rózsavölgyi Csokoládé (p71)

Vass Shoes (p71)

Getting There

Ⓜ **Metro** M3 Ferenciek tere, M1 Vörösmarty tér, M1/2/3 Deák Ferenc tér, M3/4 Kálvin tér.

🚊 **Tram** Little Ring Rd (Károly körút and Múzeum körút) for 47 or 49 from V Deák Ferenc tér to Liberty Bridge and points in south Buda; Belgrád rakpart for the 2 to V Szent István körút or southern Pest.

🚌 **Bus** V Ferenciek tere for 7 or 7E to Buda or points east in Pest; V Egyetem tér for 15 or 115 to IX Boráros tér and northern Pest.

Local Life
Exploring Váci utca & Vörösmarty tér

The capital's premier shopping street, **Váci utca** (🚊7, Ⓜ M1 Vörösmarty tér, Ferenciek tere, 🚊2) is a pedestrian strip crammed largely with chain stores, touristy restaurants and a smattering of shops and notable buildings worth seeking out. It was the total length of Pest in the Middle Ages.

1 Párisi Udvar

A good place to start is at the **Párisi Udvar** (Parisian Court; V Ferenciek tere 5; Ⓜ M3 Ferenciek tere), built in 1909. At research time, visitors could no longer glimpse the interior and its ornately decorated ceiling because it was undergoing construction, soon to be reborn as a luxury hotel. Váci utca is immediately to the west.

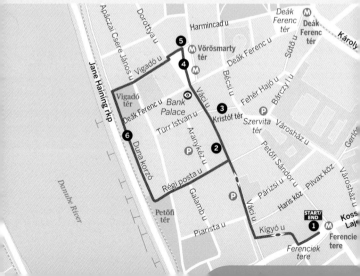

② Art Nouveau Must-Sees

Head first to **Philanthia** (V Váci utca 9; ⊙10am-7pm Mon-Thu, to 8pm Fri & Sat, 11am-6pm Sun; Ⓜ M1/2/3 Deák Ferenc tér, 🚋2), which has an original (and very rare) art nouveau interior from 1906. **Thonet House** (V Váci utca 11/a; Ⓜ M1/2/3 Deák Ferenc tér, 🚋2) is a masterpiece built by Ödön Lechner in 1890, and to the west, at Régi Posta utca 13, there's a relief of an old postal coach by the ceramicist Margit Kovács of Szentendre.

③ Fishergirl Fountain & Palace

Just off the top of Váci utca in Kristóf tér is the little Fishergirl Fountain, dating from the 19th century and complete with a ship's wheel that actually turns. A short distance to the northwest is the sumptuous **Bank Palace** (Bank Palota; V Deák Ferenc utca 3-5; Ⓜ M1 Vörösmarty tér), built in 1915 and once the home of the Budapest Stock Exchange. It has since been converted into a shopping gallery called Váci 1 and Budapest's Hard Rock Cafe.

④ Vörösmarty tér

Váci utca empties into **Vörösmarty tér** (Ⓜ M1 Vörösmarty tér), a large square of smart shops, galleries, cafes and an artist or two, who will draw your portrait or caricature. In the centre is a statue of Mihály Vörösmarty, the 19th-century poet after whom the square is named.

Shopfronts on Váci utca

⑤ Cake Stop

At the northern end of the square is **Gerbeaud** (☎1-429 9001; www.gerbeaud. hu; V Vörösmarty tér 7-8; ⊙noon-10pm; Ⓜ M1 Vörösmarty tér), Budapest's fanciest and most famous cafe and cake shop. Grab a seat on the terrace and don't fail to order the *Dobos torta,* a scrumptious layered chocolate and cream cake with a caramelised brown sugar top.

⑥ Danube Promenade

A pleasant way to return to Ferenciek tere is along the **Duna korzó** (Ⓜ M1 Vörösmarty tér, 🚋2), the riverside 'Danube Promenade' between Chain and Elizabeth Bridges.

200 m
0.1 miles

ERZSÉBETVÁROS

Holló u
Síp u
Dob u
Dohány u
Gozsdu Udvar
Rumbach Sebestyén u
Madách Imre út
Rákóczi út
Astoria
Múzeum
Magya
Kossuth Lajos u
Király u
Asboth u
Károly krt
Gerlóczy u
Semmelweiss u
Vitkovics M u
Vármegye u
Bajcsy-Zsilinszky út
Deák Ferenc tér
Underground
Railway Museum
Deák Ferenc tér
Sütő u
Bálcczy u
Pest County Hall
Városháza
Pilvax köz
Ferenciek
Municipal Council Office
Budapest Info
Fehér Hajó u
Szervita tér
Petőfi Sándor u
Harís köz
Pártisi u
BELVÁROS
13
Erzsébet tér
Október 6 u
Bécsi u
Kristóf tér
Hild tér
József Attila u
Harmincad u
Vörösmarty tér
Vörösmarty tér
Deák Ferenc u
Váci u
Aranykéz u
Türr István u
Régi posta u
Galamb
József nádor tér
Nádor u
Dorottya u
Vigadó u
Pesti Vigadó
Vigadó tér
Duna korzó
10
11
3
7
1
8
2
3
4

A
B
C
D
E
1
2
3
4

Múzeum krt

Kálvin tér

Kálvin tér

Magyar u

Lónyay u

Gönczy P u

Kecskeméti u

Királyi Pál u

Trapéz

12

Fehér György u

Veres Pálné u

Pipa u

Reáltanoda u

Ferenczy István u

Henszlmann Imre u

Papnövelde u

Szerb u

Váci u

Szentkirályi u

Só u

Fővám tér

Károlyi Mihály u

Cukor u

9

Curia u

Veres Pálné u

Nyáry Pál u

Havas u

Molnár u

Váci út

Szabadsajtó út

Duna u

Irányi u

Váci u

Molnár u

Apáczai Csere János u

6

Jane Haining rkp

International Ferry Pier

Március 15 tér

e Haining rkp

Elizabeth Bridge (Erzsébet híd)

Sights

Pesti Vigadó
NOTABLE BUILDING

 1   Map p66, A3

This Romantic-style concert hall, built in 1864 and badly damaged during WWII, faces the river to the west of Vörösmarty tér. Reopened in 2014 after reconstruction, the building has been fully restored to its former grandeur. Floors five and six have been set aside for temporary exhibitions and there's now a fantastic terrace affording expansive views over the Danube. It's a fantastic place to catch a classical concert in glamorous surrounds. English-language guided tours available (2900Ft); check the website for schedule. (www.pestivigado.hu; V Vigadó tér 1; adult/concession 2500/2000Ft; ⏱10am-7.30pm; M M1 Vörösmarty tér, 🚋2)

Trapéz
GALLERY

2   Map p66, D6

Exciting new contemporary art gallery showcasing installations, sculpture, photography and other media by up-and-coming international artists. (📞06 30 210 3120; www.trpz.hu; V Henszlmann Imre utca 3; ⏱noon-6pm Tue-Fri; M M3 Ferenciek tere, M3/4 Kálvin tér)

Underground Railway Museum
MUSEUM

3   Map p66, C2

In the pedestrian subway beneath V Deák Ferenc tér, next to the main ticket window, the small, revamped Underground Railway Museum traces the development of the capital's underground lines. Much emphasis is put on the little yellow metro (M1), continental Europe's first underground railway, which opened for the millenary celebrations in 1896. The museum is atmospherically housed in a stretch of tunnel and station, and features wonderfully restored carriages. (Földalatti Vasúti Múzeum; www.bkv.hu; Deák Ferenc tér metro station; adult/concession 350/280Ft; ⏱10am-5pm Tue-Sun; M M1/2/3 Deák Ferenc tér)

Eating

Monk's Bistrot
HUNGARIAN €€

 4   Map p66, B5

With its vaguely industrial decor, an open kitchen and young serving staff, this ambitious new restaurant specialises in bold pairings of ingredients that nevertheless seem to work, alongside contemporary re-imaginings of Hungarian dishes. The peach gazpacho with mackerel really shines, as does the beef cheek with Dijon mustard. Weekday lunch is a welcome bargain. (📞06 30 789 4718; www.monks.hu; V Piarista köz 1; mains 3980-5780Ft; 3-course lunches 2980Ft; ⏱11am-midnight; 🛜; 🚋2)

Kárpátia
HUNGARIAN €€

 5   Map p66, C5

A palace of fin-de-siècle design dating from 1877, the 'Carpathia' serves

Pesti Vigadó

almost modern Hungarian and Transylvanian specialities in both a palatial restaurant in the back and a less-expensive *söröző* (brasserie). The mostly meaty dishes are expertly prepared and the Hungarian wine list is solid. This is one place to hear authentic *csárdás* (Gypsy-style folk music), played from 6pm to 11pm. (☎1-317 3596; www.karpatia.hu; V Ferenciek tere 7-8; mains 4100-7700Ft; ⓧ11am-11pm Mon-Sat, 5-11pm Sun; 🛜🍴; Ⓜ M3 Ferenciek tere)

Magyar QTR HUNGARIAN €€

6 🍴 Map p66, B7

It's difficult not to love this bistro, for three reasons: the excellent

Hungarian wine (more than 100 vintages), the food and the fabulous river views. The succinct menu includes such inspired takes on Hungarian dishes as duck with marrow ragout and chanterelles, and Mangalica pork with truffle and blackberries. Weekly specials are based on seasonal ingredients. (☎06 70 329 7815; www.magyarqtr.com; V Belgrád rakpart 18; mains 2750-4750Ft; ⓧnoon-midnight; Ⓜ M3 Ferenciek tere, 🚋2)

Baraka FUSION €€€

7 🍴 Map p66, A1

If you only eat in one fine-dining establishment while in Budapest, make it Baraka. You're ushered into

Local Life
Károly Garden

A pleasant place to take a breather, the flora-filled **Károly Garden** (Map p66, E5; Károlyi kert; V Ferenczy István utca; **M**M3/4 Kálvin tér, 🚌47, 48, 49) was built for the Károly Palace, which now houses the **Petőfi Museum of Literature** (Map p66, D6; Petőfi Irodalmi Múzeum; 📞1-317 3611; www.pim.hu; V Károlyi utca 16; adult/6-26yr 600/300Ft, temporary exhibitions 800/400Ft; ⏱10am-6pm Tue-Sun). Frequented by locals, many with families – it has a lovely little playground – the garden is a riot of colourful flower beds in the summer months, and there are plenty of shady benches. **Csendes Társ** (Map p66, E5; 📞1-727 2100; www.facebook.com/csendestars; Magyar utca 18; ⏱11am-11pm) is an atmospheric spot for a sundowner or snack, with a little terrace of tables crowded round the park's pretty, wrought-iron entrance gate.

the monochrome dining room, where chef Norbert Bíró works his magic in the half-open kitchen. Seafood features heavily, with French, Asian and Hungarian elements to the beautifully presented dishes. The bar, with its vast array of Japanese whiskies and pan-Asian tapas, is a treat. (📞1-200 0817; www.barakarestaurant.hu; V Dorottya utca 6; mains 7200-17,500Ft, 3-course lunches 6900Ft, 7-course tasting menus 27,000Ft; ⏱11am-3pm & 6-11.30pm Mon-Sat; 🛜; **M**M1 Vörösmarty tér)

Drinking

Marionett Craft Beer House

CRAFT BEER

8 Map p66, A3

Minimalist on the inside, yet livened up by the colourful hanging marionettes, this elegant newcomer on the craft-beer scene has been winning accolades for its great selection of local brews. If you're hungry, you can nibble on sausages and pastrami sandwiches, and the drinks selection doesn't stop with beer: the wine list is excellent. Small summer terrace, too. (Marionett Kézműves Sörház; 📞06 30 832 0880; www.marionettcraftbeer.house; V Vigadó tér; ⏱3pm-midnight; **M**M1/2/3 Deák Ferenc tér, 🚌2)

Centrál Kávéház

CAFE

9 Map p66, D5

This *grande dame* of a traditional cafe dates back to 1887. Awash with leather and dark wood inside, it's also a great spot for pavement people-watching. It serves meals as well as breakfast until 11.45am (990Ft to 2950Ft), plus cakes and pastries (750Ft to 1150Ft). (📞1-266 2110; www.centralkavehaz.hu; V Károlyi utca 9; ⏱9am-11pm; 🛜; **M**M3 Ferenciek tere)

Entertainment

Akvárium Klub

LIVE MUSIC

10 Map p66, C1

The Akvárium Klub delivers a varied program of Hungarian and international live music, from indie, rock, world and pop to electronica and beyond. The main hall has capacity for 1500, the smaller for 700. There are also regular club nights here, and a bar and bistro. A carpet of drinkers layers the surrounding steps in warm weather. (☏06 30 860 3368; www.akvariumklub.hu; V Erzsébet tér; ⊗noon-1am Mon-Thu, to 4.30am Fri & Sat; Ⓜ M1/2/3 Deák Ferenc tér)

Shopping

Le Parfum Croisette   PERFUME
11 🔒 Map p66, B2

Hungary's only *parfumier*, Zsolt Zólyomi, creates scents at his atelier-shop, as well as selling cutting-edge, animal-friendly perfumes from around the globe, such as Romano Ricci's Juliette Has a Gun range of cognac scents, whose recipes go back 750 years. Zólyomi, who foresees a renaissance in the once great Hungarian perfume industry, holds perfume-making workshops here too. (☏06 30 405 0668; www.leparfum.hu; V Deák Ferenc utca 18; ⊗10am-7pm Mon-Fri, to 5pm Sat & Sun; Ⓜ M1/2/3 Deák Ferenc tér, 🚃47, 48, 49)

Rózsavölgyi Csokoládé   CHOCOLATE
12 🔒 Map p66, E6

Tiny, low-lit boutique selling delicious and artfully packaged, award-winning bean-to-bar chocolate. The range of handmade chocolates includes such

interesting flavours as coffee and balsamic vinegar, and star anise with red peppercorn. (☏06 30 814 8929; www.rozsavolgyi.com; V Királyi Pál utca 6; ⊗10.30am-1pm & 1.30-6.30pm Mon-Fri, noon-6pm Sat; Ⓜ M3/4 Kálvin tér)

Vass Shoes   SHOES
13 🔒 Map p66, B4

A traditional shoemaker that stocks ready-to-wear and cobbles to order, Vass has a reputation that goes back to 1896; some people travel to Hungary just to have their footwear made here. (☏1-318 2375; www.vass-cipo.hu; V Haris köz 2; ⊗10am-7pm Mon-Fri, to 4pm Sat; Ⓜ M3 Ferenciek tere)

 Top Tip

Budapest's Shopping Streets

Some streets or areas in Budapest specialise in certain goods or products.

Antiques V Falk Miksa utca in Pest and II Frankel Leó út in Buda.

Antiquarian and secondhand books V Múzeum körút in Pest.

Boutiques and souvenirs V Váci utca in Pest.

International fashion brands V Deák Ferenc utca (aka Fashion St) in Pest.

Local designer goods and fashion VI Király utca in Pest.

Explore

Parliament & Around

To the north of Belváros is Lipótváros (Leopold Town), with the land-mark Parliament facing the Danube to the west and the equally iconic Basilica of St Stephen to the east. You'll also discover great museums and exhibits, some lovely squares and art nouveau buildings. After dark, head east to Terézváros (Teresa Town), a neighbourhood with no shortage of lively watering holes and raving clubs.

The Sights in a Day

☀ Book the first English-language tour at the **Parliament** (p74) building. After your visit and if you feel up to it, poke your head into the **Ethnography Museum** (p80) to see how far Hungarian design has come (no judgement) from here to the galleries of Vörösmarty tér.

☀ Make your way towards Szabadság tér, stopping for lunch at **Kispiac** (p82). Admire the two art nouveau gems nearby: the **Royal Postal Savings Bank** (p80) and the **National Bank of Hungary** (p80). The **Basilica of St Stephen** (p76) is a short distance to the southeast. Visit it on your own or join a tour, and don't forget to make it up to the dome.

☽ After you've finished your pilgrimage, raise a chalice at **DiVino Borbár** (p83). For dinner you couldn't do better than head east to **Pesti Diszno** (p83). Excellent food, more good wine and you will be right on the threshold of the clubs and bars of Terézváros.

 Top Sights

Parliament (p74)

Basilica of St Stephen (p76)

♥ **Best of Budapest**

Eating

Borkonyha (p81)

Mák (p82)

Da Mario (p82)

Drinking

DiVino Borbár (p83)

Getting There

🚌 **Bus** V Szabadság tér for 15 to IX Boráros tér and northern Pest; V Deák Ferenc tér for 16 to Castle Hill and 105 to Buda.

Ⓜ **Metro** M2 Kossuth Lajos tér, M3 Arany János utca and M1, M2 and M3 Deák Ferenc tér.

🚋 **Tram** Antall József rakpart for 2 to V Szent István körút or south Pest; V Szent István körút for 4 or 6 to Buda or Big Ring Rd in Pest.

🚎 **Trolleybus** 72 and 73 from V Arany János utca to Terézváros; 70 and 78 from V Báthory utca for Erzsébetváros and City Park.

Top Sights
Parliament

Hungary's largest building, Parliament stretches for some 268m along the Danube in Pest from Kossuth Lajor tér. The choice of location was not by chance. As a counterweight to the Royal Palace high on Buda Hill on the opposite side of the river, the placement was meant to signify that the nation's future lay with popular democracy and not royal prerogative.

Országház

👁 Map p78, A4

www.hungarianparliament.com

V Kossuth Lajos tér 1-3

adult/student EU citizen 2200/1200Ft

Ⓜ M2 Kossuth Lajos tér, 🚋 2

Lion Gate & Ornamental Staircase

The main entrance is through Lion Gate on the eastern side of the building, facing recently renovated V Kossuth Lajos tér. You then ascend the sweeping 96-step Main Staircase, with frescoes by Károly Lotz and stained glass by Miksa Róth.

Domed Hall & Coronation Regalia

At the top of the stairs you enter the crown-like, 16-sided, 66m-high Domed Hall with statues of Hungary's kings on the capitals. In the centre is the Coronation Regalia, which includes the Crown of St Stephen, the nation's most important national icon, the 15th-century ceremonial sword, the orb (1301) and the oldest object among the coronation regalia: the 10th-century Persian-made sceptre, with a large crystal head depicting a lion.

Crown of St Stephen

The two-part Crown of St Stephen, with its characteristic bent cross, pendants hanging on either side and enamelled plaques of the Apostles, dates from the late 12th century and has become the very symbol of the Hungarian nation. The crown has disappeared several times over the centuries, only to later reappear. It was damaged when placed in its carrying case in the 17th century, giving it a slightly skewered look. In 1945, Hungarian fascists fleeing ahead of the Soviet army took the crown to Austria. Eventually it fell into the hands of the US army, which transferred it to Fort Knox in Kentucky. In January 1978, the crown was returned to Hungary with great ceremony – and relief.

Congress Hall

You'll also visit one of the vaulted anterooms, where political discussions take place, and the 400-seat Congress Hall, where the House of Lords of the one-time bicameral assembly sat until 1944.

☑ **Top Tips**

▶ You can join a 45-minute tour in any of eight languages; the English-language ones are usually at 10am, noon and then hourly till 4pm (and maybe at 9.15am and 9.45am as well). Book ahead, online through **Jegymester** (www.jegymester.hu).

▶ There are no tours while the National Assembly is in session.

▶ The ceremonial guards in the Domed Hall are on duty 24 hours; the guards at the flagpole outside change every hour between 8am and 7pm (earlier in winter).

✗ **Take a Break**

If you want to try authentic Hungarian sausage or salami, you're in the right part of town. **Pick Ház** (☎1-331 7783; www.pick.hu; V Kossuth Lajos tér 9; mains 425-820Ft; ◷8am-3pm Mon-Fri), selling Hungary's most celebrated brand of prepared meat, has an eat-in outlet just opposite Parliament.

Top Sights
Basilica of St Stephen

The Basilica of St Stephen is the most sacred Catholic church in all of Hungary, if for no other reason than that it contains the nation's most revered relic: the mummified right hand of the church's patron, King St Stephen. The church is also the Budapest seat of the shared Metropolitan Archdiocese of Esztergom-Budapest.

Szent István Bazilika

👁 Map p78, C7

📞 1-311 0839, 06 30 703 6599

www.basilica.hu

V Szent István tér

requested donation 200Ft

Ⓜ M3 Arany János utca

Dome

The facade of the basilica is anchored by two large **bell towers**, one of which contains a bell weighing 9.25 tonnes. Behind the towers is the 96m-high **dome** (Panoráma kilátó; ☎1-269 1849; www.basilica.hu; adult/child 500/400Ft; ⊙10am-4.30pm Oct-Jun, to 6.30pm Jul-Sep; Ⓜ M3 Arany János utca), which can be reached by a lift and 42 steps (or 302 steps if you want to walk all the way) – it offers one of the best views in the city.

Interior

The basilica's interior is rather dark and gloomy, Károly Lotz' golden **mosaics** on the inside of the dome notwithstanding. Noteworthy items include Alajos Stróbl's statue of the king-saint on the main altar and Gyula Benczúr's painting of St Stephen dedicating Hungary to the Virgin Mary and Christ Child, to the right of the main altar.

Holy Right Chapel

Behind the altar and to the left is the basilica's major drawcard: the Holy Right Chapel. It contains what is also known as the Holy Dexter, the mummified right hand of St Stephen and an object of great devotion here.

Treasury

To the right of the basilica's entrance is a small lift to the 2nd-floor treasury of ecclesiastical objects, including censers, chalices, ciboria and vestments. Don't miss the art deco double monstrance (1938). Otherwise, the treasury is a veritable shine to Cardinal Mindszenty, including his clothing, devotional objects and death mask.

☑ Top Tips

▶ Organ concerts (adult/concession from 4500/4200Ft) are held here at 8pm, usually on Tuesday, Thursday and Friday (more often in summer).

▶ If you want a good look at the Holy Right (St Stephen's mummified right hand) put 200Ft in the slot to illuminate the hand for closer inspection. (And view it from the right-hand side to see the knuckles.)

▶ English-language guided tours of the basilica (2000/1500Ft with/without dome visit) usually depart at 9.30am, 11am, 2pm and 3.30pm on weekdays and at 9.30am and 11am on Saturday, but phone or check the website to confirm.

✕ Take a Break

Cafe Kör (☎1-311 0053; www.cafekor.net; V Sas utca 17; mains 2490-4790Ft; ⊙10am-10pm Mon-Sat), just minutes away from the basilica, is a great place for lunch.

200 m
0.1 miles

ÚJLIPÓTVÁROS

Váci út

Katona József u

Kresz Géza u

Kádár u

Visegrádi u

Hegedűs Gyula u

Szent István krt

Balaton u

Falk Miksa u

Markó u

Balassi Bálint u

Széchenyi rkp

Antall József rkp

Markó u

Stollár Béla u

Szemere u

Honvéd u

Honvéd tér

Szemere u

Szalay u

Nagy Ignác u

Bihari János u

Nyugati Train Station

Nyugati pu

Nyugati tér

Jókai u

Podmaniczky u

Teréz krt

Dessewffy u

Csengery u

Lovag u

Weiner Leó u

Podmaniczky u

Nagymező u

Bajcsy-Zsilinszky út

Vadász u

Báthory u

Belváros-Lipótváros Police Station

Alkotmány u

Kálmán Imre u

LIPÓTVÁROS

Honvéd u

Valkay u

Kozma F u

Ethnography Museum

Kossuth Lajos tér

Parliament

For reviews see

◉	Top Sights	p76
◉	Sights	p80
✕	Eating	p81
◉	Drinking	p83
◉	Shopping	p83

Hungarian State
Opera House

Ⓜ **Opera**

1 ◉

Dalszínház u

Nagymező u

Ⓧ10

Ⓤ

O u

Hajós u

Lázár u

O u

Zichy Jenő u

Dessewffy u

Révay u

Paulay Ede u

Király u

Andrássy út

Podmaniczky
Frigyes tér

Ⓜ **Arany János
utca**

ász u

Nagysándor J u

Ⓧ 7

d u

Perczel M u

2 ◉ Royal Postal
Savings Bank

Bank u

National
Bank
of Hungary

3 ◉

Arany János u

**Basilica of
St Stephen**
◉

Szent István
tér

Hercegprímás u
Ⓘ 11

Sas u

Október 6 u

Ⓘ13

Bajcsy-Zsilinszky út

Ⓜ
**Bajcsy-
Zsilinszky út**

József Attila u

Ⓧ6

Erzsébet
tér

Hild
tér

József
nádor
tér

Aur…

Zoltán u

Nádor u

Steindl Imre u

Garibaldi u

Szabadság
tér
5 ◉

Széchenyi u

Akadémia u

Arany János u

Nádor u

Zrínyi u

Vigyázó Ferenc u

Ⓧ8

Mérleg u

Széchenyi
István tér

Széchenyi Chain Bridge
(Széchenyi Lánchid)

Antall József rkp

Széchenyi rkp

Eötvös
tér

5

6

7

8

A

B

C

D

E

Sights

Hungarian State Opera House
NOTABLE BUILDING

1 ◎ Map p78, E6

The neo-Renaissance Hungarian State Opera House was designed by Miklós Ybl in 1884 and is among the most beautiful buildings in Budapest. Its facade is decorated with statues of muses and opera greats such as Puccini, Mozart, Liszt and Verdi, while its interior dazzles with marble columns, gilded vaulted ceilings, chandeliers and near-perfect acoustics. If you cannot attend a performance, join one of the three daily tours. Tickets are available from the souvenir shop inside the lobby. (Magyar Állami Operaház; ☎1-332 8197; www.operavisit.hu; VI Andrássy út 22; adult/concession 2990/1990Ft; ☺tours in English 2pm, 3pm & 4pm; Ⓜ M1 Opera)

Royal Postal Savings Bank
NOTABLE BUILDING

2 ◎ Map p78, C5

East of Szabadság tér, the former Royal Postal Savings Bank is a Secessionist extravaganza of colourful tiles and folk motifs, built by Ödön Lechner in 1901. One of the most beautiful buildings in Pest, it is now part of the National Bank of Hungary. (V Hold utca 4; 🚌15)

National Bank of Hungary
NOTABLE BUILDING

3 ◎ Map p78, C6

Southeast of Szabadság tér are some of the most beautiful buildings in Pest, including the National Bank of Hungary. It has terracotta reliefs that illustrate trade and commerce through history: Arab camel traders, African rug merchants, Chinese tea salesmen and the inevitable solicitor witnessing contracts. (Magyar Nemzeti Bank; V Szabadság tér 9; 🚌15, 115)

Ethnography Museum
MUSEUM

4 ◎ Map p78, A3

Visitors are offered an easy introduction to traditional Hungarian life at this sprawling museum opposite Parliament, with thousands of displays in a dozen rooms on the 1st floor. The mock-ups of peasant houses from the Őrség and Sárköz regions of west and southwest Hungary are well done, and there are some priceless objects, which are examined through institutions, beliefs and stages of life. On the ground floor, most of the excellent temporary exhibitions deal with other peoples of Europe and further afield: Africa, Asia, Oceania and the Americas. (Néprajzi Múzeum; ☎1-473 2400; www.neprajz.hu; V Kossuth Lajos tér 12; adult/concession 1000/500Ft, with temporary exhibitions 1400/700Ft; ☺10am-6pm Tue-Sun; Ⓜ M2 Kossuth Lajos tér)

Ethnography Museum

Szabadság tér
SQUARE

5 ⊙ Map p78, B5

This square, one of the largest in Budapest, is a few minutes' walk northeast of Széchenyi István tér. As you enter you'll pass a delightful fountain that works on optical sensors and turns off and on as you approach or back away from it, as well as the controversial **Antifascist Monument** (Antifasiszta emlékmű; V Szabadság tér; 🚎15, 115, Ⓜ M2 Kossuth Lajos tér) placed here in 2014. At the northern end is a **Soviet Army memorial** (V Szabadság tér; Ⓜ M2 Kossuth Lajos tér), the last of its type still standing in the city. (Liberty Square; 🚎15, Ⓜ M2 Kossuth Lajos tér)

Eating

Borkonyha
HUNGARIAN €€

6 ✗ Map p78, C8

Chef Ákos Sárközi's approach to Hungarian cuisine at this Michelin-starred restaurant is contemporary, and the menu changes every week or two. Go for the signature foie gras appetiser wrapped in strudel pasty and a glass of sweet Tokaj wine. If *mangalica* (a special type of Hungarian pork) is on the menu, try it with a glass of dry *furmint*. (Wine Kitchen; 📞1-266 0835; www.borkonyha.hu; V Sas utca 3; mains 3150-7950Ft; 🕒noon-4pm & 6pm-midnight Mon-Sat; 🚎15, 115, Ⓜ M1 Bajcsy-Zsilinszky út)

Kispiac
HUNGARIAN €€

7 Map p78, C5

This hole-in-the-wall retro-style restaurant next to the Belvárosi Piac market on Hold utca serves *seriously* Hungarian things like stuffed *csülök* (pig's trotter – and way better than it sounds), roast *malac* (piglet) and an infinite variety of *savanyúság* (pickled vegetables). There's a warm welcome, and you probably won't eat again for a week. (☑1-269 4231; www.kispiac.eu; V Hold utca 13; mains 2300-3950Ft; ◷noon-10pm Mon-Sat; MM3 Arany János utca)

Mák
INTERNATIONAL €€

8 Map p78, A7

The award-winning 'Poppy' serves inventive international dishes that lean in the direction of Hungary from a chalkboard menu that changes daily. Casual surrounds and seamless and very friendly service, with good advice on wine. At lunch the menu's two/three courses are a budget-friendly 3200/3800Ft. (☑06 30 723 9383; www.mak.hu; V Vigyázó Ferenc utca 4; mains 3400-6800Ft; ◷noon-3pm & 6pm-midnight Tue-Sat; ☐15, 115, ☐2)

Da Mario
ITALIAN €€

9 Map p78, B5

Owned and operated by a southern Italian, Da Mario can't put a foot wrong in our book. While the cold platters, soups, and meat and fish mains all look good, we stick to the house-made pasta dishes (2000Ft to 3500Ft) and pizzas (2000Ft to 4200Ft) from the wood-burning stove. (☑1-301 0967; www.damario.hu; V Vécsey utca 3; mains 2000-6000Ft; ◷11am-midnight; ☐15, 115, MM2 Kossuth Lajos tér)

Understand
Garden Clubs & Ruin Bars

- -

During the long and often very hot summers, so-called *kertek* (literally 'gardens', but in Budapest any outdoor spot that has been converted into an entertainment zone) empty out even the most popular indoor bars and clubs. These vary enormously, from permanent bars with an attached garden, and clubs with similar outdoor sections, to totally alfresco spaces only frequented in good weather.

Ruin pubs (*romkocsmák*) began to appear in the city from the early 2000s, when entrepreneurial free thinkers took over abandoned buildings and turned them into pop-up bars. At first a very word-of-mouth scene, the ruin bars' popularity grew exponentially and many have transformed from ramshackle, temporary sites full of flea-market furniture to more slick, year-round fixtures with covered areas.

Pesti Disznó

HUNGARIAN €€

10 Map p78, E5

Punters would be forgiven for thinking that the 'Pest Pig' was all about pork. In fact, of the 10 main courses more than half are poultry, fish or vegetarian. It's a wonderful space, loft-like almost, with high tables and charming, informed service. The wine card is very, very good and most wines are available by the glass, too. (1-951 4061; www.pestidiszno.hu; VI Nagymező utca 19; mains 2690-4490Ft; 11am-midnight Sun-Wed, to 1am Thu-Sat; ; M M1 Oktogon)

Drinking

DiVino Borbár

WINE BAR

11 Map p78, C7

Central and always heaving, DiVino is Budapest's most popular wine bar, as the crowds spilling out onto the square in front of the Basilica of St Stephen in the warm weather will attest. Choose from more than 140 wines produced by three dozen winemakers under the age of 35, but be careful: those 0.15dL glasses (650Ft to 3500Ft) go down quickly. (06 70 935 3980; www.divinoborbar.hu; V Szent István tér 3; 4pm-midnight Sun-Wed, to 2am Thu-Sat; M M1 Bajcsy-Zsilinszky út)

Alterego

GAY

12 Map p78, E5

Still Budapest's premier gay club, Alterego has the chicest crowd and the best dance music on offer. Don't miss the drag shows by Lady Dömper and the Alterego Trans Company. Always a hoot. (06 70 565 1111; www.alterego-club.hu; VI Dessewffy utca 33; 10pm-5am Fri, to 6am Sat; 4, 6)

Local Life

Antique Browsing

One of our favourite places to while away part or all of a Saturday morning is along V Falk Miksa utca, which is lined with antique and curio shops. Start at the northern end with **BÁV** (Map p78, B1; Bizományi Kereskedőház és Záloghitel; 1-473 0666; www.bav.hu; XIII Szent István körút 3; 10am-7pm Mon-Fri, to 2pm Sat; 4, 6) and end up at the largest of them all: **Pintér Galéria** (Map p78, A2; 1-311 3030; www.pinterantik.hu; V Falk Miksa utca 10; 10am-6pm Mon-Fri, to 2pm Sat; 2, 4, 6).

Shopping

Bestsellers

BOOKS

13 Map p78, B7

Our favourite English-language bookshop in town, with fiction, travel guides and lots of Hungarica, as well as a large selection of newspapers and magazines overseen by master bookseller Tony Láng. Helpful staff are at hand to advise and recommend. (1-312 1295; www.bestsellers.hu; V Október 6 utca 11; 9am-6.30pm Mon-Fri, 11am-6pm Sat, noon-6pm Sun; M M1/2/3 Deák Ferenc tér)

Explore

Margaret Island & Northern Pest

Neither Buda nor Pest, 2.5km-long Margaret Island (Margit-sziget) lies in the middle of the Danube. The island is not overly endowed with important sights and landmarks, but you can easily spend half a day exploring its swimming complexes, thermal spa, gardens, centuries-old Turkish and other ruins. To the east, Újlipótváros (New Leopold Town) is full of tree-lined streets and perfect for lunch or coffee.

The Sights in a Day

☼ Revisit Budapest's medieval past on Margaret Island by strolling or cycling among the ruins of the **Franciscan church and monastery** (p87), one-time **Dominican convent** (p87) where St Margaret is buried and the **Premonstratensian Church** (p88).

☀ For a panoramic view of the island, climb the steps of the Lookout Gallery at the **Water Tower** (p88), then cross over Margaret Bridge and stop by **Édesmindegy** (p89) for top-notch cakes and afternoon sweet treats.

☾ Continue up Pozsonyi út to pay homage to the heroic Raoul Wallenberg at his statue in **Szent István Park** (p89). Have dinner at **Firkász** (p90) and spend the rest of the evening at the incomparable **Budapest Jazz Club** (p91).

 Best of Budapest

Eating

Laci! Konyha! (p89)

Oriental Soup House (p89)

Drinking

Double Shot (p90)

Getting There

🚋 **Tram** Both districts served by trams 4 and 6. Tram 2 to XIII Jászai Mari tér from the Inner Town.

🚌 **Bus** 26 covers the length of Margaret Island running between Nyugati train station and Árpád Bridge. Újlipótváros via bus 15 and 115.

🚎 **Trolleybus** 75 and especially 76 are excellent for Újlipótváros.

Ⓜ **Metro** The eastern end of Újlipótváros is best reached by metro (M3 Nyugati train station).

A   B   C   D

ÚJLAK

Árpád fejedelem útja

1

Premonstratensian
Church **4**

Palatinus
Strand
5 Water Tower &
7 Open-Air Theatre

Szépvölgyi út

Duna River

Hajós Alfréd sétány

Dominican
Convent **3**

VÍZAFOGÓ

Népfürdő u

Révész u

For reviews see
◉ Sights   p87
✗ Eating   p89
🅟 Drinking   p90
★ Entertainment   p91
🛍 Shopping   p91

2
Franciscan
Church and
Monastery

Margaret Island
(Margit-sziget)

Dráva u

Dózsa
György Ⓜ
György

Tisza u

László u

Hegedüs Gyula u

Vág u

Tutaj u

Alfél

Kárpát u

Bessenyei u

Garam u

Gogol u

Visegrádi u

Carl Lutz rkp

Ipoly u

Thurzó u

Röntgen u

Kassák La

Kassák D

Szent
István
Park

10 ✗

Hollán Ernő u

Pozsonyi út

Victor Hugó u

Csanády u

Lehel
tér Ⓜ

Leh

6 ◉

8 ✗

Tátra u

Pannónia u

Lehel
tér

ÚJLIPÓTVÁROS

Margit híd

Margaret
Bridge
1 ◉

12 🅟
🅟 ✗ **9**

11 ✗

Radnóti Miklós u

Balzac u

Ferdinánd híd

13 🅟

Katona József u

15 🛍 **14**

Jászai
Mari tér

Tátra u

Visegrádi u

Kresz Géza u

Váci út

WestEnd
City Centre

Szent István krt

Antall József rkp

Kádár u

Nyugati
tér

Podmaniczk

Balaton u

LIPÓTVÁROS

Nyugati pu Ⓜ

Nyugati
Train Station

N 0   500 m
   0   0.25 miles

Franciscan Church & Monastery

Sights

Margaret Bridge
BRIDGE

1 ◉ Map p86, A4

Margaret Bridge, which has finally emerged from a massive three-year reconstruction, introduces the Big Ring Rd to Buda. It's unique in that it doglegs in order to stand at right angles to the Danube where it converges at the southern tip of Margaret Island. The bridge was originally built by French engineer Ernest Gouin in 1876; the branch leading to the island was added in 1901. (Margit híd; 🚊2, 4, 6)

Franciscan Church & Monastery
RUINS

2 ◉ Map p86, B2

These ruins – no more than a tower and a wall dating to the late 13th century – are in the centre of the island. Habsburg Archduke Joseph built a summer residence here when he inherited the island in 1867. It was later converted into a hotel, which operated until 1949. (Ferences templom és kolostor; 🚊26)

Dominican Convent
RUINS

3 ◉ Map p86, B1

A ruin is all that remains of the 13th-century convent built by Béla

Understand
St Margaret

The island's most famous resident was Béla IV's daughter Margaret (1242–71). The king supposedly pledged her to a life of devotion in a nunnery if the Mongols, who had overrun Hungary in 1241–42, were expelled. They were and she was – at age nine. Still, she seemed to enjoy it (if we're to believe *Lives of the Saints*), especially the mortification-of-the-flesh parts. Canonised only in 1943, St Margaret commands something of a cult following in Hungary.

IV where his daughter St Margaret (1242–71) lived. According to the story, the king promised to commit his daughter to a life of devotion in a nunnery if the Mongols were driven from the land. They were and she was – at nine years of age. A red-marble sepulchre cover surrounded by a wrought-iron grille marks her original resting place and there's a viewpoint overlooking the ruins. Canonised in 1943, St Margaret commands something of a cult following in Hungary. A short distance southeast of th e sepulchre there's a much-visited brick shrine with votives thanking her for various favours and cures. (Domonkos kolostor; 🚇26)

Premonstratensian Church
CHURCH

4 ◎ Map p86, C1

This reconstructed Romanesque Premonstratensian Church, dedicated to St Michael by the order of White Canons, dates back to the 12th century. Its 15th-century bell mysteriously appeared one night in 1914 under the roots of a walnut tree knocked over in a storm. It was probably buried by monks during the Turkish invasion. (Premontre templom; 🚇26)

Water Tower & Open-Air Theatre
ARCHITECTURE

5 ◎ Map p86, B1

Erected in 1911 in the north-central part of Margaret Island, the octagonal water tower rises 66m above the **open-air theatre** (*szabadtéri színpad*), which is used for concerts and plays in summer. The tower contains the **Lookout Gallery** (Kilátó Galéria). Climbing the 153 steps will earn you a pleasant 360-degree view of the island, consisting mostly of treetops. En route you'll see a recent exhibition of Budapest landscapes being projected on to bare walls. (Víztorony és Szabadtéri Színpad; 📞06 20 383 6352; Lookout Gallery adult/concession 600/300Ft; ⊙Lookout Gallery 11.30am-7pm May-Oct; 🚇26)

Szent István Park PARK

6 Map p86, B4

St Stephen Park contains a statue of
Raoul Wallenberg doing battle with
a snake (evil). Erected in 1999 and
titled *Kígyóölő* (Serpent Slayer), it is
a copy of the one created by sculptor
Pál Pátzay that was removed by the
communist regime in 1949. Facing the
river is a row of Bauhaus apartments,
which were the delight of modern-
ists when they were built in the late
1920s. Enter from the southern end.
(Szent István körút; Újpesti rakpart; ⊗8am-
8pm; ☐15, ☐trolleybus 75, 76)

Palatinus Strand SWIMMING

7 Map p86, B1

The largest and best series of outdoor pools in the capital, the 'Palatinus Beach' complex has upward of
a dozen pools (two with thermal
water), wave machines, water slides
and kids' pools. (☑1-340 4505; www.
palatinusstrand.hu; XIII Margit-sziget; adult/
child Mon-Fri 2800/2100Ft, Sat & Sun
3200/2300Ft; ⊗9am-7pm May-Sep; ☐26)

Eating

Oriental
Soup House VIETNAMESE €

8 Map p86, C4

Though it's far away from central
Budapest, this authentic Vietnamese
joint is regularly packed. Customers squeeze around the communal

tables beneath paper lanterns and
tuck into several kinds of *pho* (rice
noodle soup), as well as *mien ga*
(chicken noodle soup) and *bun cha*
(grilled pork and noodles). (☑06
70 617 3535; www.facebook.com/oriental-
souphouse; XIII Hollán Ernő utca 35; mains
750-1990Ft; ⊗11.30am-10pm Sun-Thu, to
11pm Fri & Sat; ☑; ☐trolleybus 75, 76)

Édesmindegy CAFE €

9 Map p86, B4

Come here for some of Budapest's
best and most imaginative cakes.
Temptations include poppy-seed
cheesecake with almond and sea
buckthorn, strawberry cheesecake
with Sichuan pepper, chocolate tart
with salted caramel and probably
the best *pasteis de nata* (custard

Top Tip

Cycle the Island

Margaret Island is bigger than you think, so rent a bicycle or other wheeled equipment from **Bringóhintó** (Map p86, B1; [📞]1-329 2073; www.bringohinto.hu; per 30/60min mountain bikes 690/990Ft, pedal coaches for 4 people 2280/3680Ft; [🕑]8am-dusk; [🚌]26), at the refreshment stand near the **Japanese Garden** (Map p86, B1; Japánkert; [🚌]26) in the northern part of the island.

tarts) outside Portugal. ([📞]06 30 502 9358; www.facebook.com/Edesmindegy; XIII Pozsonyi út 16; cakes 1090Ft; [🕑]9am-9pm; [🚌]4, 6)

Sarki Fűszeres

CAFE €

10 Map p86, C3

This delightful retro-style cafe on tree-lined Pozsonyi út is the perfect place for brunch, a late breakfast, a specialty coffee or just a quick sandwich. Doubles as a deli/wine shop. (Grocery Store on Corner; [📞]1-238 0600; www.facebook.com/sarkifuszeres; XIII Pozsonyi út 53-55; breakfast & sandwiches 790-2300Ft; [🕑]8am-8pm Mon-Fri, to 3pm Sat; [🚋]trolleybus 75, 76)

Firkász

HUNGARIAN €€

11 Map p86, B4

Set up by former journalists, retro-style restaurant 'Hack' has been one of our favourite Hungarian 'nostalgia' eateries for years, thanks to the lovely old mementos on the walls, great homestyle dishes such as roast goose leg in red wine and Karpati-style pike-perch, a good wine list and nightly piano music. ([📞]1-450 1118; www.firkasz.hu; XIII Tátra utca 18; mains 2390-7990Ft; [🕑]noon-midnight; [🚌]15, 115, [🚊]4, 6)

Drinking

Double Shot

COFFEE

12 🔴 Map p86, B4

With an unfinished, grungy look, and break-your-neck stairs to the small seating area upstairs, this thimble-sized coffee shop is the brainchild of two expats. The artisan coffee from around the globe is excellent. ([📞]06 70 674 4893; www.facebook.com/doubleshotspecialtycoffee; XIII Pozsonyi út 16; [🕑]7am-8pm Mon-Thu, 7am-9pm Fri, 8am-9pm Sat, 8am-7pm Sun; [🚊]4, 6)

L.A. Bodegita

COCKTAIL BAR

13 🔴 Map p86, B4

The Cuban-style food here is missable, but you should definitely taste master mixologist András Lajsz' incomparable American-style (hi, LA!) cocktails; he does a mean Cosmo and we also take the Chameleon, the house special. Live Cuban music on Friday night. ([📞]1-789 4019; www.labodegita.hu; XIII Pozsonyi utca 4; cocktails 1400-1900Ft; [🕑]11am-midnight

Couple by the river with bikes

Mon-Wed, to 2am Thu-Sat, to 6pm Sun; 🚎trolleybus 75, 76, 🚊2, 4, 6)

Hollán Ernő utca 7; 🕙10am-midnight Sun-Thu, to 2am Fri & Sat; 🚎trolleybus 75, 76)

Entertainment

Budapest Jazz Club   JAZZ

14 ⭐ Map p86, B4

A very sophisticated venue – now pretty much the most serious one in town – for traditional, vocal and Latin jazz by local and international talent. Past international performers have included Terrence Blanchard, the Yellowjackets and Liane Carroll. Concerts most nights at 8pm or 9pm, with jam sessions at 10pm or 11pm on Friday, Saturday and Monday. (📞1-798 7289; www.bjc.hu; XIII

Shopping

Mézes Kuckó   FOOD

15 🔒 Map p86, B4

This hole-in-the-wall is the place to go if you have the urge for something sweet; its nut-and-honey cookies, 240Ft per 10 decagrams (100g), are to die for. A colourfully decorated *mézeskalács* (honey cake; 330Ft to 750Ft) in the shape of a heart makes a lovely gift. (Honey Nook; XIII Jászai Mari tér 4; 🕙10am-6pm Mon-Fri, 9am-1pm Sat; 🚊2, 4, 6)

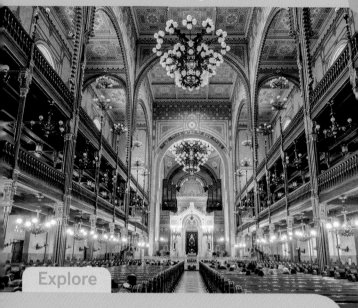

Explore

Erzsébetváros & the Jewish Quarter

This neighbourhood takes in Erzsébetváros (Elizabeth Town) and most of Terézváros, including well- and high-heeled Andrássy út, the long, dramatic and very chic boulevard that slices through Terézváros. It hosts a large percentage of Budapest's accommodation at all levels, restaurants serving everything from Chinese and Indian vegetarian to French and Serbian, and the city's hottest nightspots.

The Sights in a Day

☼ Spend the morning exploring the old Jewish Quarter by following our Erzsébetváros & the Jewish Quarter walk. You'll take in both the **Great Synagogue** (p94) and the **Hungarian Jewish Museum & Archives** (p95). On the way to Klauzál tér, the heart of this district, have a look at the **Orthodox Synagogue** (p101), almost austere after the flamboyance of the main temple.

☼ Grab some lunch at **Bors Gasztro Bár** (p102) before making your way to the city's stately boulevard, **Andrássy út** (p100). Stroll south and visit the **House of Terror** (p100). Veer off slightly to check out the **Ferenc Liszt Memorial Museum** (p101).

☾ Have dinner at the **Spinoza Café** (p103), especially if it's Friday and the *klezmer* musicians are performing. Otherwise, check out some of the neighbourhood's best bars and clubs by following the Bar-Hopping in Erzsébetváros tour.

For a local's day in Erzsébetváros, see p96.

◉ Top Sights
Great Synagogue (p94)

◯ Local Life
Bar-Hopping in Erzsébetváros (p96)

♥ Best of Budapest
Eating
Spinoza Café (p103)

Fröhlich Cukrászda (p95)

Drinking
Doblo (p103)

Lotz Terem Book Cafe (p104)

Shopping
Massolit Budapest (p106)

Printa (p106)

Getting There

Ⓜ **Metro** Three metro lines converge at Deák Ferenc tér, handy for western Erzsébetváros. Oktogon is on the M1 metro line and Blaha Lujza tér is on the M2 and M4; also useful are the M2 and M4 Astoria and Keleti train stations.

🚊 **Tram** VII Erzsébet körút for 4 or 6 to Buda or the rest of Big Ring Rd in Pest.

🚎 **Trolleybus** VII Wesselényi utca and Dohány utca for 74 to Little Ring Rd or City Park.

Top Sights
Great Synagogue

Budapest's stunning Great Synagogue, with its crenellated red-and-yellow glazed-brick facade and two enormous Moorish-style towers, is the largest Jewish house of worship in the world outside New York City, seating 3000 worshippers. Built in 1859, the copper-domed Conservative (not Orthodox) synagogue contains both Romantic-style and Moorish architectural elements. It is also called the Dohány utca Synagogue (Dohány utcai Zsinagóga).

Nagy Zsinagóga

⊙ Map p98, B8

www.dohany-zsinagoga.hu

VII Dohány utca 2

adult/concession incl museum 3000/2000Ft

Ⓜ M2 Astoria, 🚋 47, 49

Rose Window

Because some elements of the synagogue recall Christian churches – including the central rose window with an inscription from the second book of Moses – the synagogue is sometimes referred to as the 'Jewish cathedral'. It was renovated in the 1990s largely due to private donations, including US$5 million from the cosmetic magnate Estée Lauder, who was born in New York to Hungarian Jewish immigrants.

Interior Fittings

Don't miss the decorative carvings on the Ark of the Covenant by National Romantic architect Frigyes Feszl, who also did the wall and ceiling frescoes of multicoloured and gold geometric shapes. Both Franz Liszt and Camille Saint-Saëns played on the rebuilt 5000-pipe organ dating back to 1902. Concerts are held here in summer.

Hungarian Jewish Museum & Archives

The Hungarian Jewish Museum & Archives, upstairs in an annexe of the synagogue, contains objects related to religious and everyday life. Interesting items include 3rd-century Jewish headstones from Roman Pannonia discovered in 1792 in Nagykanizsa in southwestern Hungary, a vast amount of liturgical items in silver, and manuscripts, including a handwritten book of the local Burial Society from the late 18th century.

Holocaust Tree of Life Memorial

In **Raoul Wallenberg Memorial Park** on the synagogue's north side and opposite VII Wesselényi utca 6, the Holocaust Tree of Life Memorial, designed by Imre Varga in 1991, stands over the mass graves of those murdered by the Nazis in 1944–45. On the leaves of the metal 'tree of life' are the family names of some of the hundreds of thousands of victims.

☑ Top Tips

▶ A 2½-hour walking tour (adult/student 6900/6500Ft) of the Jewish Quarter departs from the Great Synagogue at 10am Sunday to Friday and at 2pm Monday to Thursday.

▶ A plaque on the Great Synagogue notes that Tivadar (Theodore) Herzl, the father of modern Zionism, was born on the site in 1860.

▶ Get one of the free audioguides available in a dozen languages; labelling in the Hungarian Jewish Museum is poor.

✗ Take a Break

Have lunch at Spinoza Café (p103), which, though not kosher, serves Jewish specialties as well as an excellent-value all-day breakfast.

For something sweet – and kosher – head for **Fröhlich Cukrászda** (www.frohlich.hu; VII Dob utca 22; ⊙9am-6pm Mon-Thu, to 2pm Fri, 10am-6pm Sun). Its *flódni* (a three-layer cake) is legendary.

Local Life
Bar-Hopping in Erzsébetváros

Wander along Király utca or down Gozsdu udvar on a Friday night and it can feel like the whole world and their best friend are here. Jostling with wide-eyed tourists and hen and stag parties may leave you wondering whether the locals have deserted this area altogether. They haven't – you just need to know where to find them.

❶ Sample a Hungarian Craft Beer

Tiny **Csak a jó sör** (☎ 06 30 251 4737, 1-950 2788; www.csakajosor.hu; VII Kertész utca 42-44; ⏱ 2-9pm Mon-Sat; Ⓜ M1 Oktogon, 🚋 4, 6) closes early, so it's a good place to start your evening. True to the name, which translates as 'only good beer', the shelves of this tiny shop are stacked high with brown bottles containing an extensive selection of international bottled craft beer. Another half-dozen

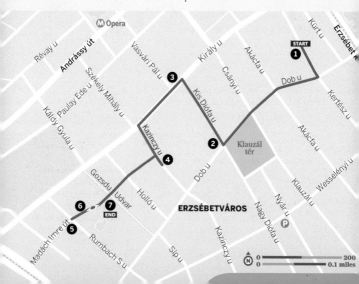

are usually on draught. Nearby is its sister pub **Hopaholic** (☎1-611 2415; www. facebook.com/hopaholicpub; VII Akácfa utca 38; ☾4pm-midnight Mon-Wed, to 2am Thu-Sat;, which keeps longer hours.

② Check Out a Little Local Bar

With your appetite whetted, it's a short hop to **Kisüzem** (Map p98, C6; ☎06 20 957 2291, 1-781 6705; www.facebook.com/Kisuzem; VII Kis Diófa utca 2; ☾noon-Sun-Wed, to 3am Thu-Sat; ☎; ☒4, 6), where relaxed drinkers hang out on the bar's little outside benches. Head inside to check out what live jazz, folk and experimental music is on the agenda.

③ Taste Some Hungarian Wine

On bustling Király utca, **Kadarka** (☎06 30 297 4974, 1-266 5094; www.facebook.com/ kadarkabar; VII Király utca 42; ☾4pm-midnight; ☎; ⓜM1 Opera) offers a huge list of Hungarian wines in a modern, sociable bar. Take a table on the street for a spot of people-watching, or settle on a tall bar stool inside and settle for some advice from the ever-helpful servers.

④ Hang Out in a Garden Club

At **Mika Tivadar Mulató** (Map p98, B6; ☎06 20 965 3007; www.mikativadarmulato. hu; VII Kazinczy utca 47; ☾4pm-midnight Sun-Wed, to 3am Thu-Sat; ⓜM1/2/3 Deák Ferenc tér), just around the corner, you'll find a chilled ground-floor bar, a small venue downstairs and a fantastic garden courtyard, which is among our favourite *romkertek* (ruin gardens) in Budapest. In the fairy-lit garden, take a seat in the boat and enjoy a drink adrift in a sea of chattering locals.

⑤ Stroll Bar-Lined Streets

Down the road, Madách Imre út is usually packed. Numerous bars line the pedestrian alley, but locals favour **Központ** (☎1-783 8405; www.facebook. com/kozpontbudapest; VII Madách Imre út 5; ☾8am-1am Mon-Wed, to 2am Thu & Fri, 6pm-2am Sat; ⓜM1/2/3 Deák Ferenc tér), which is the hipster meeting place in Budapest where bearded young men gather by night to drink, chat and listen to canned music. If feeling peckish pop next door to **Igen** (Map p98, A7; ☎06 20 348 0132; www.facebook.com/igenitalia; slices 380-580Ft, pizzas 1520-2320Ft; ☾noon-midnight Tue-Thu, to 2am Fri & Sat, to 10pm Sun) for some of the best pizza in town.

⑥ Listen to Live Music

Further south on Madách Imre út is **Telep** (☎1-784 8911; www.facebook.com/TelepGaleria; VII Madách Imre út 8; ☾noon-2am Mon-Fri, 4pm-2am Sat; ☎), an exhibition space and art gallery, wallpapered with stickers and hosting nightly live music or DJs. If the weather's warm, the street will be filled with folk hanging out on the pavement with a beer.

⑦ Head to a Club

If you're ready to ramp things up a bit, head back towards Gozsdu udvar, where the basement club at **Gozsdu Manó Klub** (GMK; Map p98, B7; ☎06 20 779 1183; www.gozsdumano.hu; VII Gozsdu udvar, cnr Madách Imre út; ☾4pm-2am Sun-Wed, to 5am Thu-Sat; ⓜM1/2/3 Deák Ferenc tér) has an excellent sound system and a good reputation for quality DJs and live music.

400 m
0.2 miles

Lendvay u

Munkácsy Mihály u

Bajza u

Bajza utca Ⓜ

Szondi u

Bajza u

Bajza utca

Benczúr u

Városligeti fasor

Székely Bertalan u

Kodály körönd Ⓜ

Kodály körönd

Felső erdősór

Lövölde tér

Szinyei Merse u

Aradi u

Kmetty György u

Andrássy út

Rottenbiller u

Rózsa u

Izabella u

Josika u

Bajnok u

Szív u

Aradi u

✕ 8

Podmaniczky u

Rózsa u

Szófia u

Király u

Ferenc Liszt Memorial Museum

Hunyadi tér

★ 23

Ⓜ Vörösmarty utca

★ 4

Izabella u

Vörösmarty u

Csengery u

Vörösmarty utca

House of Terror ◉ 2

Csengery u

Ferdinánd híd

Szondi u

Eötvös u

Oktogon Ⓜ Oktogon

Eötvös u

Podmaniczky u

TERÉZVÁROS

Csengery u

Teréz krt

Jókai tér

Szobi u

Teréz krt

Mozsár u

Ⓟ

Jókai u

Zichy Jenő u

Dessewffy u

Jókai u

Weiner L u

Lovag u

Nagymező u

Ⓟ Nyugati Train Station

Nyugati tér Ⓜ Nyugati pu

Jókai u

Hajós u

Bajcsy-Zsilinszky út

Sights

Andrássy út
ARCHITECTURE

1 Map p98, B5

Andrássy út starts a short distance northeast of Deák Ferenc tér and stretches for 2.5km, ending at Heroes' Sq (Hősök tere) and the sprawling City Park (Városliget). Recognised by Unesco as a World Heritage Site in 2002, it is a tree-lined parade of knock-out architecture and is best enjoyed as a long stroll from the Hungarian State Opera House (p80) out to the park. (M̄ M1 Opera)

House of Terror
MUSEUM

2 Map p98, C3

The main headquarters of the dreaded secret police is now the startling House of Terror, focusing on the crimes and atrocities of Hungary's fascist and Stalinist regimes in a permanent exhibition called Double Occupation. But the years after WWII leading up to the 1956 Uprising get the lion's share of the exhibition space (almost three-dozen spaces on three levels). The reconstructed prison cells in the basement and the Perpetrators' Gallery, featuring photographs of the turncoats, spies and torturers, are absolutely chilling. (Terror Háza; ☎1-374 2600; www.terrorhaza.hu; VI Andrássy út 60; adult/concession 2000/1000Ft, audioguide 1500Ft; ⏱10am-6pm Tue-Sun; M̄ M1 Oktogon)

Liszt Music Academy
NOTABLE BUILDING

3 Map p98, C5

The art nouveau Liszt Music Academy, built in 1907, attracts students from all over the world and is a top concert venue (Liszt Zeneakadémia; ☎1-462 4600, box office 1-321 0690; www.zeneakademia.hu; VI Liszt Ferenc tér 8; ⏱box office 10am-6pm; M̄ M1 Oktogon, 📢4, 6). The renovated interior, which has five concert halls and is richly embellished with Zsolnay porcelain and frescoes, is worth visiting on a guided tour if you're not attending a performance. (Liszt Zeneakadémia; ☎1-462 4600; www.zeneakademia.hu; VI Liszt Ferenc tér 8; adult/concesssion 7500/3750Ft; ⏱daily tours 1.30pm; M̄ M1 Oktogon, 📢4, 6)

 Top Tip

Little Underground

The M1 metro (aka Kisföldalatti; Little Underground), which runs just below Andrássy út from Deák Ferenc tér as far as City Park, sticks to its side of the road below the surface and there's no interchange between the two sides. So, if you're heading north, board the trains on the east side of Andrássy út; for points south, the west side. Also possibly confusing is that one station is called Vörösmarty tér and another, five stops away, is Vörösmarty utca.

House of Terror

Ferenc Liszt Memorial Museum

MUSEUM

4 Map p98, D3

This wonderful little museum is housed in the Old Music Academy, where the great composer lived in a first-floor apartment for five years until his death in 1886. The three rooms are filled with his pianos (including a tiny glass one), portraits and personal effects – all original. Concerts (adult/child 1500/750Ft or 2200/1000Ft with a museum visit) are usually held in the Chamber Hall at 11am on Saturday. (Liszt Ferenc Emlékmúzeum; 1-322 9804; www.lisztmuseum.hu; VI Vörösmarty utca 35; adult/child 1500/750Ft;

⏱10am-6pm Mon-Fri, 9am-5pm Sat; M M1 Vörösmarty utca)

Orthodox Synagogue

SYNAGOGUE

5 Map p98, C7

Once one of a half-dozen synagogues and prayer houses in the Jewish Quarter, the Orthodox Synagogue was built in 1913 in what was at the time a very modern design. It has late art nouveau touches and is decorated in bright colours throughout. The stained-glass windows in the ceiling were designed by Miksa Róth, although what you see today are reconstructions, as the originals were bombed during WWII. (Ortodox zsinagóga; ☏1-351 0524; www.kazinczy-utcaizsinagoga.hu; VII Kazinczy utca 29-31; 1000Ft; ⊙10am-6pm Sun-Thu, to 4pm Fri Apr-Oct, 10am-4pm Sun-Thu, to 2pm Fri Nov-Mar; MM2 Astoria, ☐47, 49)

Eating

Bors Gasztro Bár   SANDWICHES €

 6 ☒ Map p98, C7

We love this thimble-sized place, not just for its hearty, imaginative soups (how about sweet potato with coconut or tiramisu?) but for its equally good grilled baguettes: try 'Bors Dog' (spicy sausage and cheese) or 'Brain Dead' (pig's brains are the main ingredient). It's not a sit-down kind of place; most chow down on the pavement outside. (www.facebook.com/BorsGasztroBar; VII Kazinczy utca 10; soups 600Ft, baguettes 670-890Ft; ⊙11.30am-midnight; ✐; MM2 Astoria)

Igen   PIZZA €

7 ☒ Map p98, A7

We'll always say 'Yes' (the meaning of *igen*) to this tiny pizzeria near Gozsdu udvar that features four regular pizzas (margherita, marinara, potato and truffle) and four 'guest' ones. It's Italian-owned and -operated, and the pizzas are as authentic as you'd find in Naples, Italy. (☏06 20 348 0132; www.facebook.com/igenitalia; VII Madách Imre út 5; slices 380-580Ft, pizzas 1520-2320Ft; ⊙noon-midnight Tue-Thu, to 2am Fri & Sat, to 10pm Sun; MM1/2/3 Deák Ferenc tér)

Zeller Bistro   HUNGARIAN €€

 8 ☒ Map p98, D4

You'll receive a very warm welcome at this lovely candlelit cellar where the attentive staff serve food sourced largely from the owner's family and friends in the Lake Balaton area. The Hungarian home cooking includes some first-rate dishes such as grey beef, duck leg, oxtail and lamb's knuckle. Superb desserts too. Popular with both locals and expats; reservations are essential. (☏1-321 7879, 06 30 651 0880; VII Izabella utca 38; mains 2900-5400Ft; ⊙noon-3pm & 6-11pm Tue-Sat; MM1 Vörösmarty utca, ☐4, 6)

Kőleves   JEWISH €€

9 ☒ Map p98, B6

Always buzzy and lots of fun, the 'Stone Soup' attracts a young crowd with its Jewish-inspired (but not kosher) menu, lively decor, great service and reasonable prices. Good vegetarian choices. Breakfast (890Ft to 1250Ft) is served from 8am to 11.30am. The daily lunch is just 1250Ft, or 1100Ft for the vegetarian version. (☏06 20 213 5999; www.kolevesvendeglo.hu; VII Kazinczy utca 37-41; mains 2120-4920Ft; ⊙8am-1am Mon-Fri, 9am-1am Sat & Sun; ☎✐; MM1/2/3 Deák Ferenc tér)

Barack & Szilva   HUNGARIAN €€

 10 ☒ Map p98, D7

This is the kind of perfectly formed restaurant that every neighbourhood wishes it could boast. Run by a husband-and-wife team, the 'Peach & Pear' serves high-quality and exceptionally well-prepared Hungarian provincial food in a bistro setting. Try the duck pâté with dried plums and the red-wine beef *pörkölt* (goulash). Lovely terrace in summer too. (☑1-798 8285; www.barackesszilva.hu; VII Klauzál utca 13; mains 3200-5500Ft; ◷6pm-midnight Mon-Sat; Ⓜ M2 Blaha Lujza tér)

M Restaurant   HUNGARIAN €€

 11 Map p98, C5

A small, romantic spot with laid-back vibe, a brown-paper-bag decor and a short but very well thought-out menu of Hungarian dishes with a French twist. Recommended. (☑06 70 633 3460, 1-322 3108; www.metterem.hu; VII Kertész utca 48; mains 2200-3200Ft; ◷6pm-midnight; ⊙; Ⓜ M1 Oktogon, ◻4, 6)

Spinoza Café   HUNGARIAN €€

 12 Map p98, B7

This attractive cafe-restaurant includes an art gallery and theatre, where *klezmer* (Jewish folk music) concerts are staged at 7pm on Fridays (9500Ft with three-course meal), along with a coffee house and restaurant where there's live piano music nightly. The food is mostly Hungarian and Jewish comfort food, not kosher but no pork. The all-day breakfast (1500Ft) is a steal. (☑1-413 7488; www.spinozacafe.hu; VII Dob utca 15; mains 1950-4650Ft; ◷8am-midnight Mon-Fri, 9am-11.30pm Sat & Sun; Ⓜ M2 Astoria)

Drinking

Szimpla Kert   RUIN PUB

 13 Map p98, C7

Budapest's first *romkocsmá* (ruin pub), Szimpla Kert is firmly on the drinking-tourists' trail but remains a landmark place for a drink. It's a huge complex with nooks filled with bric-a-brac, graffiti, art and all manner of unexpected items. Sit in an old Trabant car, watch a film in the open-air back courtyard, down shots or join in an acoustic jam session. (☑06 20 261 8669; www.szimpla.hu; VII Kazinczy utca 14; ◷noon-4am Mon-Thu & Sat, 10am-4am Fri, 9am-5am Sun; Ⓜ M2 Astoria)

Doblo   WINE BAR

14 Map p98, B7

Brick-lined and candlelit, Doblo is where you go to taste Hungarian wines, with scores available by the 1.5cL glass for 900Ft to 2150Ft. There's food too, such as meat and cheese platters. (www.budapestwine.com; VII Dob utca 20; ◷1pm-2am Sun-Wed, 1pm-4am Thu-Sat; Ⓜ M1/2/3 Deák Ferenc tér)

Boutiq' Bar   COCKTAIL BAR

15 Map p98, A6

A low-lit 'speakeasy' serving expertly mixed cocktails (2250Ft to 5950Ft) using fresh juices and an educated selection of craft spirits. For something specifically Hungarian, try a creation that includes Unicum like Die Kaiser, or plum *pálinka* (fruit brandy) such

Szimpla Kert (p103)

as Positive Drinking. The gin-based Budapest BBQ is something else. Informed, charming service; reservations are advised. (📞06 30 554 2323; www.boutiqbar.hu; V Paulay Ede utca 5; ⏰6pm-1am Tue-Thu, to 2am Fri & Sat; Ⓜ M1 Bajcsy-Zsilinszky utca)

Kisüzem
BAR

16 Ⓠ Map p98, C6

The bare-brick interior of this relaxed corner bar gives it a bohemian vibe. A mixed-age crowd mingles at the bar or on the pavement outside, or chats at the tables ranged around the interior. It hosts live music such as jazz, folk and experimental (usually at 9pm Thursday and Sunday), and serves bar food and locally roasted coffee. (📞06 20 957 2291, 1-781 6705; www.facebook.com/Kisuzem; VII Kis Diófa utca 2; ⏰noon-2am Sun-Wed, to 3am Thu-Sat; 🛜; 🚊4, 6)

Lotz Terem Book Cafe
CAFE

17 Ⓠ Map p98, B5

On the 1st floor of a branch of Alexandra, one of Budapest's best bookshops, this glitzy cafe in the revamped decorative hall of the one-time Paris Department Store shows off frescoes by Károly Lotz and other wonderful touches of opulence. It's a great spot for a light lunch (salads and sandwiches; 1290Ft to 2590Ft) or for coffee pre- or post-browse. (📞1-461 5835; www.lotzterem.hu; VI Andrássy út 39; 🕙10am-8pm; Ⓜ M1 Opera, 🚊4, 6)

Mika Tivadar Mulató   CLUB

18 Ⓣ Map p98, B6

This grand one-time copper factory dating from 1907 sports a chilled ground-floor bar, a small venue downstairs and a fantastic garden courtyard, among our favourite *romkertek* (ruin gardens) in Budapest. Most nights there are DJs and live music (all sorts, including jazz, swing, punk and funk). Great toilets. (📞06 20 965 3007; www.mikativadarmulato. hu; VII Kazinczy utca 47; 🕙4pm-midnight Sun-Wed, to 3am Thu-Sat; Ⓜ M1/2/3 Deák Ferenc tér)

Instant   CLUB

19 Ⓣ Map p98, C6

We still love this 'ruin bar' on one of Pest's most vibrant nightlife strips and so do all our friends. It has 26 rooms, seven bars, seven stages and two gardens with underground DJs and dance parties. It's always heaving. (📞1-311 0704, 06 30 830 8747; www. instant.co.hu; VII Akácfa utca 51; 🕙4pm-6am; Ⓜ M1 Opera)

Gozsdu Manó Klub   CLUB

20 Ⓣ Map p98, B7

There's an upstairs bar and res-taurant here, but the real draw is the basement club, which puts on

excellent live music and DJs in a cavernous space with a quality sound system, an unpretentious vibe and a devoted local following. (GMK; 📞06 20 779 1183; www.gozsdumano.hu; VII Gozsdu udvar, cnr Madách Imre út; 🕙4pm-2am Sun-Wed, to 5am Thu-Sat; Ⓜ M1/2/3 Deák Ferenc tér)

CoXx Men's Bar   GAY

21 Ⓣ Map p98, C7

Probably the cruisiest gayme in town, this place with the in-your-face name has 400 sq metres of hunting ground, three bars and some significant play areas in back. Don't bring dark glasses. (📞06 30 949 1650, 1-344 4884; www.coxx.hu; VII Dohány utca 38; 🕙9pm-4am Sun-Thu, to 5am Fri & Sat; Ⓜ M2 Blaha Lujza tér, 🚊4, 6)

Entertainment

Gödör   LIVE MUSIC

22 ⭐ Map p98, A7

In the bowels of the Central Passage shopping centre on Király utca, Gödör has maintained its reputation for scheduling an excellent variety of indie, rock, jazz, electronic and experimental music, as well as hosting quality club nights in its spare, industrial space. Exhibitions and movies in summer too. (📞06 20 201 3868; www.godorklub.hu; VI Király utca 8-10, Central Passage; 🕙6pm-late; 📶; Ⓜ M1/2/3 Deák Ferenc tér)

Q Local Life
Szimpla Farmers Market

Every Sunday, Budapest's original ruin pub Szimpla Kert (p103) holds a charming **farmers market** (Map p98, C7; www.szimpla.hu; VII Kazinczy utca 14; ◷9am-2pm Sun; 🛜; ⓂM2 Astoria), where you can buy all manner of locally produced jam, honey, yoghurt, cheese and bread. Also available are paprika, vegetables, fruit, cured meat and fruit juice.

Budapest Puppet Theatre

PUPPET THEATRE

23 ⭐ Map p98, D3

The city's puppet theatre presents shows designed for children at 10am or 10.30am, and 2.30pm or 3pm. Performances usually don't require fluency in Hungarian. Consult the website for program schedules and exact times. (Budapest Bábszínház; ☎1-321 5200, box office 1-342 2702; www.budapest-babszinhaz.hu; VI Andrássy út 69; tickets 1300-1900Ft; ◷box office 9am-6pm; ⓂM1 Vörösmarty utca)

Shopping

Massolit Budapest

BOOKS

24 🔒 Map p98, C7

A branch of the celebrated bookshop in Kraków, Massolit is one of Budapest's best, with new and secondhand English-language fiction and nonfiction, including Hungarian history and literature in translation. It has a beautiful shady garden and tables set among the shelves, so you can enjoy coffee, sandwiches, cakes and bagels as you browse the volumes. (☎1-788 5292; www.facebook.com/MassolitBudapest; VII Nagy Diófa utca 30; ◷8am-7.30pm Mon-Sat, 10am-7.30pm Sun; ⓂM2 Astoria)

Gouba

MARKET

25 🔒 Map p98, B7

A weekly arts and crafts market along Gozsdu udvar, where you can pick up some interesting pieces from local artists and designers. It's a good place to shop for souvenirs, too. (www.gouba.hu; VII Gozsdu udvar; ◷10am-7pm Sun; ⓂM1/2/3 Deák Ferenc tér)

Printa

FASHION & ACCESSORIES

26 🔒 Map p98, B7

This wonderful, hip silkscreen studio, design shop and gallery focuses on excellent local talent and sells beautiful bags, leather goods, prints, T-shirts, stationery and jewellery. There's both recycled and upcycled clothing too. (☎06 30 292 0329; www.printa.hu; VII Rumbach Sebestyén utca 10; ◷11am-7pm Mon-Sat; ⓂM1/2/3 Deák Ferenc tér)

Understand

The Jews of Budapest

Jews can trace their presence in Hungary and the area that is now Budapest to at least the 3rd century AD – well before the arrival of the Magyars. Over the centuries, Jews underwent the usual roller-coaster ride of toleration and oppression. They were blamed for the plague and expelled by King Louis the Great (Nagy Lajos) in 1360, but then they were readmitted and prospered under good King Matthias Corvinus and even the Ottoman Turks. With full emancipation after the 1867 Compromise, Jews dominated the burgeoning middle class during Budapest's Golden Age at the end of the 19th century.

White Terror

After the failure of the communist Republic of Councils under Béla Kun (himself a Jew) in 1919, Miklós Horthy launched his 'white terror' and Jews again became the scapegoats. Life was not easy for Jews under Horthy between the wars, but they were not deported to Germany. But when Hitler removed Horthy from power and installed the Hungarian pro-Nazi Arrow Cross Party, deportations began. During the summer of 1944, a mere 10 months before the war ended, 60% of Hungarian Jews were sent to Auschwitz and other labour camps, where they were murdered or died from abuse.

Jewish contribution to life here, always great, has continued into the 21st century, and the music scene is particularly lively in Budapest. Several restaurants serve kosher food, even more serve non-kosher Jewish dishes, and there are four active synagogues. Today Hungary's Jews (not necessarily claiming to be religious) number about 80,000, down from a prewar population of more than 10 times that. Almost 90% live in Budapest.

Ongoing Anti-Semitism

But while there has been a revival of Jewish culture in Budapest, there has also been a resurgence of openly expressed anti-Semitism. In November 2012, Márton Gyöngyösi, an MP for the far-right Jobbik party, called for the government to compile a national list of Hungarian Jews, whom he described as a 'national security risk' for alleged solidarity with Israel. Despite the outrage caused by this remark, the party's stances remain popular with voters. Jobbik polled 20% of the vote in the April 2014 parliamentary election.

Explore

Southern Pest

The colourful districts of Józsefváros (Joseph Town) and Ferencváros (Francis, or Franz, Town) are traditionally working class and full of students. It's a lot of fun wandering the backstreets, peeping into courtyards and small, often traditional, shops. Both are ever-changing and developing areas, with new shops, bars and restaurants popping up constantly.

The Sights in a Day

☀ Begin the day wandering the backstreets between the **Nagycsarnok** (p112; pictured left) and **Rákóczi tér market** (p113). Then spend an hour or two in the **Hungarian National Museum** (p110); the exhibits relating to the 1956 Uprising will help put what you've seen on your walk into perspective.

☀ In the afternoon, ogle the spectacular art nouveau tiles and furniture at the **Museum of Applied Arts** (p115). Carry on to the **Holocaust Memorial Center** (p116). If you're lucky there will be a temporary exhibition in the courtyard's lovingly restored synagogue.

☾ Have a stiff drink at **Élesztő** (p117) and contemplate the evening's possibilities. A curry or thali at **Curry House** (p116) makes for a nice change after all that pork and paprika. Spend the rest of the night grooving at **Corvin Club & Roof Terrace** (p117), one of our favourite Budapest clubs.

For a local's day in Southern Pest, see p112.

 Top Sights

Hungarian National Museum (p110)

 Local Life

From Market to Market (p112)

💜 **Best of Budapest**

Drinking
Corvin Club & Roof Terrace (p117)

Élesztő (p117)

Museums & Galleries
Museum of Applied Arts (p115)

Getting There

Ⓜ **Metro** Key stops include Blaha Lujza tér and Keleti train station on the M2, Corvin-negyed on the M3, Rákóczi tér on the M4, and Kálvin tér, where the M3 and M4 intersect.

🚋 **Tram** Both districts are served by trams 47 and 49, and further east by trams 4 and 6.

Top Sights
Hungarian National Museum

The Hungarian National Museum houses the nation's most important collection of historical relics. It traces the history of the Carpathian Basin from the Stone Age and that of the Magyar people and Hungary from the 9th-century conquest to the end of communism. The museum was founded in 1802 when Count Ferenc Széchényi donated his personal collection to the state.

Magyar Nemzeti Múzeum

👁 Map p114, B2

www.hnm.hu

VIII Múzeum körút 14-16

adult/concession 1600/800Ft

🕑10am-6pm Tue-Sun

🚊47, 49, Ⓜ M3/4 Kálvin tér

Front Steps
Less than a year after it moved into its new premises, an impressive neoclassical building, designed by Mihály Pollack in 1847, the museum was the scene of a momentous event. On 15 March a crowd gathered to hear the poet Sándor Petőfi recite his 'Nemzeti Dal' (National Song) from the front steps, sparking the 1848–49 revolution.

Archaeological Exhibition
Exhibits on the 1st floor trace the history of the Carpathian Basin and its peoples from earliest times to the end of the Avar period in the early 9th century. Don't miss the Golden Stag, a hand-forged Iron Age figure from the 6th century BC once part of a Scythian prince's shield. On the lower level just beyond the entrance is a stunning 2nd-century Roman mosaic from Balácapuszta, near Veszprém.

Coronation Mantle
In its own room to the left on the 1st floor, you'll find King Stephen's beautiful crimson silk coronation mantle, stitched by nuns in 1031. It was refashioned in the 13th century and the much-faded cloth features an intricate embroidery of fine gold thread and pearls.

Museum Gardens
You may enjoy walking around the museum gardens, laid out in 1856. The Roman column to the left of the museum entrance once stood at the Forum and was a gift from Mussolini. Among the monuments is a statue of János Arany (1817–82), author of the epic *Toldi Trilogy*. There's also a Soviet tank dating from 1956.

☑ Top Tips
▶ Audioguides for the permanent collection are available in English for 750Ft for the first hour and 250Ft after that.

▶ The museum shop sells excellent reproductions of 3rd-century Celtic gold and silver jewellery.

▶ Should you be in the area on National Day (15 March), expect a lot of pomp and circumstance as Petőfi's reading of his 'National Song' is re-enacted on the museum's front steps.

✖ Take a Break
The **Építész Pince** (☎1-266 4799; www.epiteszpince.hu; VIII Ötpacsirta utca 2; mains 2050-4250Ft; ⊙11am-10pm Mon-Thu, to midnight Fri & Sat), just round the corner, serves a bargain set lunch from Monday to Friday.

If you just want a drink, head east to Mikszáth Kálmán tér and Lumen (p117) for some of the best coffee and local craft beers in town.

Local Life
From Market to Market

The ideal way to appreciate these two fascinating but large traditionally working-class districts is to pick a sight and then spend some time wandering in the nearby streets. We've chosen an area between two great markets that is filled with antiquarian bookshops, ghosts from the 1956 Uprising, unusual architecture and trendy bars and restaurants.

....

1 Nagycsarnok

The **Nagycsarnok** (Great Market Hall; ☎1-366 3300; www.piaconline.hu; IX Vámház körút 1-3; ⏱6am-5pm Mon, to 6pm Tue-Fri, to 3pm Sat; Ⓜ M4 Fővám tér) is Budapest's largest market. It might attract tourists in droves, but it's always a hive of activity and a great place for one-stop shopping. Gourmets will appreciate the Hungarian and other treats available here for

less than they'd pay in the shops on nearby Váci utca – shrink-wrapped and potted foie gras, garlands of dried paprika, souvenir sacks and tins of paprika powder, and as many kinds of honey as you'd care to name.

❷ Brunch Break

Ráday utca, a long strip whose pavement tables fill with diners on warm summer days, is a lively place to head to in this district at any time of day. Stop for brunch at **Jedermann Cafe** (📞 06 30 406 3617; www.jedermann.hu; XI Ráday utca 58; 🕙 8am-1am; 📶; 🚋 4, 6), an uber-chilled cafe and restaurant at the southern end of the street.

❸ Antiquarian Bookshop

The western side of Múzeum körút is lined with shops selling antiquarian and secondhand books. Our favourite is **Múzeum Antikvárium** (📞 1-317 5023; www.muzeumantikvarium.hu; V Múzeum körút 35; 🕙 10am-6pm Mon-Fri, to 2pm Sat; Ⓜ M3/4 Kálvin tér) just opposite the Hungarian National Museum. Further north is **Központi Antikvárium** (📞 1-317 3514; www.kozpontiantikvarium.hu; V Múzeum körút 13-15; 🕙 10am-6pm Mon-Fri, to 2pm Sat; Ⓜ M2 Astoria), the largest and oldest in town.

❹ Brody House

Now a fancy-schmancy hotel, Brody House would have lots of tales to tell could it speak. It was the residence of Hungary's prime minister in the 19th century when Parliament sat next door at No 8. And if you don't believe that, look at the verso of the 20,000Ft note.

❺ Former Hungarian Radio Headquarters

On the evening of 23 October 1956, ÁVH government agents fired on a group of protesters gathering outside these **radio headquarters** (Magyar Rádió; VIII Bródy Sándor utca 5-7; Ⓜ M3 Kálvin tér, 🚌 47, 49) when they began shouting anti-Soviet slogans and demanding that reformist Imre Nagy be named prime minister. By morning Budapest was in revolution.

❻ Rákóczi tér Market

Rákóczi tér has sported this handsome and very authentic **market hall** (📞 1-476 3921; www.piaconline.hu; VIII Rákóczi tér 7-9; 🕙 6am-4pm Mon, to 6pm Tue-Fri, to 1pm Sat; Ⓜ M4 Rákóczi tér, 🚋 4, 6) since 1897. Inside you'll find all the usual staples – fruit, veg, cured meats, cheese, jam and baked goods – and some folk bring their goods up direct from the farm.

❼ Coffee at the 'Snail'

Finish off your day at **Café Csiga** (Cafe Snail) (📞 06 30 613 2046; www.facebook.com/cafecsiga; VIII Vásár utca 2; 🕙 9am-midnight; 📶; Ⓜ M4 Rákóczi tér, 🚋 4, 6), a relaxed space just opposite the market, with battered wooden floorboards, copious plants and wide-open doors on sunny days. The Snail does food, too, including lots of vegetarian options, breakfast and an excellent set lunch (1100Ft).

400 m
0.2 miles

A — Károly krt

Kossuth Lajos u

Szép u
Reáltanoda u
Ferenczy István u

Egyetem tér

Szerb u

Veres Pálné u

Váci u

Fővám tér
Fővám tér

Danube River

Dohány u
Rákóczi út
Puskin u
Trefort u
Szentkirályi u

Bródy Sándor u

Magyar u

Kecskeméti u

Bástya u

Kálvin tér

Kálvin tér

Göncz y Pu

Pipa u

Csarnok tér Imre u

Lónyay u

Czuczor u

Kinizsi u

Mátyás u

Erkel u

Köztelek u

Markusovszky tér

Ráday u

Bakáts u

Bakáts tér

Köztelek u

Klauzál u

Blaha Lujza tér

Bezerédj u

Vas u
Gyulai Pál u
Stáhly u
Somogyi B u

8

Horánszky u
Mária u
Rökk Szilárd u
Gutenberg tér
Bérkocsis u

József krt

Rákóczi tér

Déri Miksa u
Vig u
Német u

Bacsó Béla utca
Tolnai Lajos u
Népszínház u

Múzeum u

Mikszáth Kálmán tér
Lőrinc pap tér

Szabó Ervin tér

Ervin Szabó Central Library

Baross u

Csepreghy u

Pál u

Museum of Applied Arts

Corvin-negyed

Üllői út

Kis Stáció u
Horvá Mihály
Rigó u

József krt

Kisfaludy u
Nap u

Práter u

Vajdahunyad u

Futó u

Nap u

Tűzoltó u

Holocaust Memorial Center

Tompa u

Angyal u

Liliom u

Liliom u

Mester u

Ferenc krt

Bakáts u

Köztelek u

Ráday u

Kinizsi u

Knézich u

Hőgyes E U

Ferenc tér
Balázs Bé

Bokréta u

Berzenczey u

Boráros tér

9

4

11

Petőfi Bridge
(Petőfi híd)

Kőzraktár u

Hungarian National Museum

Kálvin tér

Fővám tér

7

5

10

3

1

Museum of Applied Arts

Sights

Museum of Applied Arts

MUSEUM

1 Map p114, C4

The Museum of Applied Arts, housed in a gorgeous Ödön Lechner–designed building (1896) decorated with Zsolnay ceramic tiles, has two permanent collections. One contains Hungarian and European furniture from the 18th and 19th centuries, art nouveau and Secessionist artefacts, and objects relating to trades and crafts (glassmaking, bookbinding, goldsmithing). The other consists of Islamic art and artefacts from the 9th to the 19th centuries. (Iparművészeti Múzeum; www.imm.hu; IX Üllői út 33-37; adult/student 2000/1000Ft, with temporary exhibitions 3500/1750Ft; ⏱10am-6pm Tue-Sun; Ⓜ M3 Corvin-negyed, 🚊4, 6)

Kerepesi Cemetery

CEMETERY

2 Map p114, D1

Budapest's equivalent of London's Highgate or Père Lachaise in Paris, this 56-hectare necropolis was established in 1847 and holds some 3000 gravestones and mausoleums, including those of statesmen and national heroes Lajos Kossuth, Ferenc Deák and Lajos Batthyány. Maps with the location of noteworthy graves are available free at the entrance. Plot 21 contains the graves of many who died in the 1956 Uprising. (Kerepesi temető;

www.nemzetisirkert.hu; VIII Fiumei út 16; admission free; ⊙7am-8pm May-Jul, to 7pm Apr & Aug, to 6pm Sep, to 5pm Mar & Oct, 7.30am-5pm Nov-Feb; Ⓜ M2/4 Keleti train station, 🚌24)

Ervin Szabó Central Library

LIBRARY

3 Map p114, B3

Southeast of the Hungarian National Museum is the main repository of Budapest's public library system, which holds 2.4 million books and bound periodicals and upwards of 250,000 audiovisual and digital items. Completed in 1889, the public reading room has gypsum ornaments, gold tracery and enormous chandeliers. It's worth quickly registering (with photo ID) to gain access, but you can just visit the cafe to get a sense of the building. (Fővárosi Szabó Ervin Könyvtár; www.fszek.hu; VIII Reviczky utca 1; admission free; ⊙10am-8pm Mon-Fri, to 4pm Sat; Ⓜ M3/4 Kálvin tér)

Holocaust Memorial Center

JEWISH SITE

4 Map p114, D4

Housed in a striking modern building, the Holocaust Memorial Center opened in 2004, on the 60th anniversary of the start of the Holocaust in Hungary. The thematic permanent exhibition traces the rise of anti-Semitism in Hungary and follows the path to genocide of Hungary's Jewish and Roma communities. A sublimely restored synagogue in the central courtyard (1924), designed by Leopold Baumhorn, hosts temporary exhibitions, while an 8m wall nearby bears the names of Hungarian victims of the Holocaust. (Holokauszt Emlékközpont; www.hdke.hu; IX Páva utca 39; adult/concession 1400/700Ft; ⊙10am-6pm Tue-Sun, Ⓜ M3 Corvin-negyed, 🚌4, 6)

Eating

Curry House

INDIAN €

5 Map p114, C2

This richly decorated and well-run Indian restaurant offers a warm welcome, attentive service, and a wide range of authentic dishes. There are lots of options for vegetarians (1300Ft to 2200Ft) as well as lunchtime thalis (trays with a variety of tasting-size dishes), succulent tandoori (1700Ft to 3000Ft) and accomplished curries. (🕿1-264 0297; www.curryhouse.hu; VIII Horánszky utca 1; mains 1700-3100Ft; ⊙11am-10pm Tue-Sun; 🍴; Ⓜ M4 Rákóczi tér)

Rosenstein

HUNGARIAN €€

6 Map p114, D1

A top-notch and cosy Hungarian restaurant in an unlikely location, with Jewish tastes and super service. Family-run – the owner is also the chef – it has been here for years, so expect everyone to know each other. The extensive menu features some interesting game dishes as well as good-value daily lunch specials (2200Ft to 3200Ft). (🕿1-333 3492; www.rosenstein.hu; VIII Mosonyi utca 3; mains 2900-6500Ft; ⊙noon-11pm Mon-Sat; Ⓜ M2/4 Keleti train station, 🚌24)

Múzeum HUNGARIAN €€€

 7 Map p114, B2

This cafe-restaurant is the place to come if you like to dine in old-world style with a piano softly tinkling in the background. It's still going strong after 130 years at the same location. The goose-liver parfait (3400Ft) is to die for, the goose leg and cabbage (3900Ft) iconic. There's also a good selection of Hungarian wines. (☏1-267 0375; www. muzeumkavehaz.hu; VIII Múzeum körút 12; mains 3600-7200Ft; ⊙6pm-midnight Mon-Sat, noon-3pm Sun; Ⓜ M3/4 Kálvin tér)

Drinking

Corvin Club & Roof Terrace CLUB

8 Map p114, C1

On top of the former Corvin department store, this excellent club, with stunning views from its open-air dance floor, holds a variety of nights from techno to rooftop cinema. If you can't face the stairs, once you've paid (cover 500Ft to 2000Ft) head 100m south to the Cafe Mundum at Somogyi Béla utca 1 and ride the goods lift to the roof. (www.corvinteto.hu; VIII Blaha Lujza tér 1; ⊙10pm-6am Wed-Sat; Ⓜ M2 Blaha Lujza tér)

Élesztő CRAFT BEER

9 Map p114, D4

This ruin pub, set in a former glass-blowing workshop, has three sections: a cafe, a wine bar with tapas (690Ft to 1390Ft) and the reason we come...a bar with an unrivalled selection of craft beer. With a brewery on-site and a name meaning 'yeast', 20 brews on tap, beer cocktails and brewing courses, this is a hophead's dream. (www. facebook.com/elesztohaz; IX Tűzoltó utca 22; ⊙3pm-3am; Ⓜ M3 Corvin-negyed, 🚋4, 6)

Lumen CAFE

10 Map p114, C2

A relaxed cafe bar with a terrace on Mikszáth Kálmán tér, this joint roasts its own coffee and serves wine and Hungarian craft beer like Stari. In the evenings it fills with an arty crowd who come for the eclectic program of live music and DJ nights. (www.facebook.com/ lumen.kavezo; VIII Mikszáth Kálmán tér 2-3; ⊙8am-midnight Mon-Fri, 10am-midnight Sat, 10am-10pm Sun; 🛜; Ⓜ M3/4 Kálvin tér, 🚋4, 6)

Entertainment

Palace of Arts CONCERT VENUE

11 ⭐ Map p114, C5

The two concert halls at this palatial arts centre by the Danube are the 1700-seat Béla Bartók National Concert Hall and the smaller Festival Theatre, accommodating up to 450 people. Both are purported to have near-perfect acoustics. Students can pay 500Ft one hour before all performances for a standing-only ticket. (Művészetek Palotája; ☏1-555 3300; www.mupa.hu; IX Komor Marcell utca 1; ⊙box office 10am-6pm; 🛜; 🚋2, 24, 🚈HÉV 7 Közvágóhíd)

Top Sights
City Park

Getting There

M The M1 metro from Vörösmarty tér to Hősök tere and Széchenyi fürdő.

No 70 from V Kossuth Lajos tér, 72 from V Arany János utca and 75 from XIII Jászai Mari tér.

City Park is a heavyweight when it comes to Budapest's top sights. Apart from one world-class art museum and a smaller one dedicated to contemporary art, there's also Budapest's most impressive square, not to mention the zoo, Széchenyi Baths and a fine 19th-century castle. By 2019 City Park's roster of attractions is due to include a biodome, a new amusement park, a new art gallery to house the Hungarian National Art collection and a revamped Transport Museum.

Hosok Tere (Millennium Monument), Heroes' Square

Museum of Fine Arts

The **Museum of Fine Arts** (Szépművészeti Múzeum; ☑1-469 7100; www.mfab.hu; XIV Dózsa György út 41; Ⓜ M1 Hősök tere), in a neoclassical building on the northern side of Heroes' Sq, houses the city's most outstanding collection of foreign works of art dating from antiquity to the 21st century. The nucleus of the collection dates back to 1870, when the state purchased the private collection of Count Miklós Esterházy. It's currently closed, due to reopen in 2018.

Széchenyi Baths

The gigantic 'wedding cake' of a building in City Park dates from just before the outbreak of WWI and houses the **Széchenyi Baths** (Széchenyi Gyógyfürdő; ☑1-363 3210; www.szechenyibath.hu; XIV Állatkerti körút 9-11; tickets incl locker/cabin Mon-Fri 4700/5200Ft, Sat & Sun 4900/5400Ft; ⊙6am-10pm; Ⓜ M1 Széchenyi fürdő), whose hot-water spring was discovered while a well was being drilled in the late 19th century. It also stands out for its immensity (it's the largest medicinal bath extant in Europe, with 15 indoor pools and three outdoor).

Heroes' Square & Millenary Monument

Heroes' Sq is the largest and most symbolic **square** (Hősök tere; ☐105, Ⓜ M1 Hősök tere) in Budapest, and contains the Millenary Monument (Ezeréves emlékmű), a 36m-high pillar topped by a golden Archangel Gabriel. Legend has it that he offered Stephen the crown of Hungary in a dream. At the column's base are Prince Árpád and other chieftains. The colonnades behind the pillar feature various illustrious leaders of Hungary. It was designed in 1896 to mark the 1000th anniversary of the Magyar conquest of the Carpathian Basin.

☑ **Top Tips**

▶ For lofty views of the park's iconic architecture and beyond, it's well worth taking a guided tour up the newly opened **Apostles' Tower** (Apostolok Tornya; www.mezogazdasagimuzeum.hu; Vajdahunyadvár; 600Ft; ⊙10am-5pm Tue-Sun; Ⓜ M1 Széchenyi fürdő).

▶ At the museum, don't try to see everything in one visit: pick a couple of collections and enjoy them in depth.

▶ At Széchenyi, for a cheaper bathing experience visit after 5pm.

✖ **Take a Break**

If it's Sunday head for **Gundel** (www.gundel.hu; XIV Gundel Károly út 4; mains 5500-59,000Ft; set lunch menus 5900-7500Ft, Sun brunch adult/child 7900/3950Ft; ⊙noon-midnight; ⓪) and its famous brunch. **Robinson** (www.robinsonrestaurant.hu; XIV Városligeti tó; mains 4000-13,700Ft; ⊙11am-11pm, restaurant noon-3pm & 6-11pm; ⓪) is a good place for a lakeside drink or light meal.

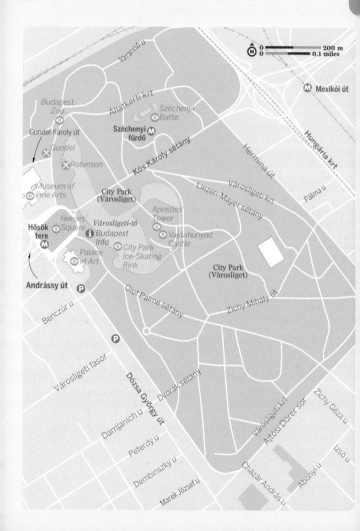

Budapest Zoo

This **zoo** (Budapesti Állatkert; ☎1-273 4900; www.zoobudapest.com; XIV Állatkerti körút 6-12; adult/2-14yr/family 2500/1800/7300Ft; ☺9am-6pm Mon-Thu, to 7pm Fri-Sun; 🚼; 🚋trolleybus 72, Ⓜ M1 Széchenyi fürdő), which opened with 500 animals in 1866, has an excellent collection of big cats, hippopotamuses, bears and giraffes, and some of the themed houses (eg Madagascar, wetlands, nocturnal Australia) are well executed, though water in ponds could be less stagnant. Have a look at the Secessionist animal houses built in the early part of the 20th century, such as the Elephant House with Zsolnay ceramics, and the Palm House with an aquarium erected by the Eiffel Company of Paris.

Palace of Art

The **Palace of Art** (Műczarnok; www.mucsarnok.hu; XIV Dózsa György út 37; adult/concession 1800/900Ft; ☺10am-6pm Tue, Wed & Fri-Sun, noon-8pm Thu; 🚌20, 30, Ⓜ M1 Hősök tere), reminiscent of a Greek temple, is among the city's largest exhibition spaces. It focuses on contemporary visual arts, with some three to four major exhibitions staged annually; recent exhibitions comprised cutting-edge photography, sculpture and installations by home-grown and international artists. Go for the scrumptious venue and the excellent museum shop. Concerts are sometimes staged here as well.

> ### Understand
> #### Unknown Chronicler
> ------------
> The statue of the hooded figure opposite Vajdahunyad Castle is that of Anonymous, the unknown chronicler at the court of King Béla III who wrote a history of the early Magyars. Note the pen with the shiny tip in his hand; writers (both real and aspirant) stroke it for inspiration.

Vajdahunyad Castle

Built for the 1896 millenary celebrations, the **castle** (Ⓜ M1 Széchenyi fürdő) was modelled after a fortress in Transylvania – but with Gothic, Romanesque and baroque wings and additions to reflect architectural styles from all over Hungary.

Ice-Skating Rink

In late November or early December, the western edge of the lake in City Park, in the shadow of Vajdahunyad Castle, becomes Europe's largest outdoor **skating rink** (Városligeti Műjégpálya; ☎06 20 261 5209; www.mujegpalya.hu; XIV Olof Palme sétány 5; ☺9am-1pm & 5-9pm Mon-Fri, 10am-2pm & 4-9pm Sat & Sun late Nov–Feb; Ⓜ M1 Hősök tere). Skates are available for hire (800Ft per hour). If you want to avoid the crowds, visit on a weekday morning.

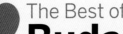

The Best of
Budapest

Budapest's Best Walks

Budapest's Best...

Panoramic view of Budapest
ROMAN SIGAEV/SHUTTERSTOCK ©

Best Walks
Castle Hill

🏃 The Walk

There's no better introduction to Budapest than a tour of Castle Hill. The neighbourhood has everything that defines this delightful city: history, architecture, fabulous views and tourists in spades. If you'd like to take in the first three but avoid the last, make this an early-morning walk.

Start Ⓜ II Széll Kálmán tér

Finish Ⓜ II Clark Ádám tér

Length 1.2km; two hours

🍴 Take a Break

You might have to linger for a seat, but **Ruszwurm Cukrászda** (p124), established in 1827, is perfect for coffee and cake. Another sweet stop option is **Budavári Rétesvár** (p124), serving all kinds of strudel.

National Archives

❶ Vienna Gate

Walk up Várfok utca from Széll Kálmán tér to **Vienna Gate**, the medieval entrance to the Old Town, rebuilt in 1936 to mark the 250th anniversary of the retaking of the castle from the Turks. It's not that huge, but when loquacious Hungarian children natter on, their parents tell them: 'Be quiet, your mouth is as big as the Vienna Gate!'

❷ National Archives

The large building to the west with the superbly coloured majolica-tiled roof contains the **National Archives** (Országos Levéltár), completed in 1920. Note the attractive group of burgher houses across Bécsi kapu tér, site of a weekend market in the Middle Ages.

❸ Táncsics Mihály utca

Narrow **Táncsics Mihály utca** is full of little houses painted in lively hues and adorned with statues. In many courtyard entrances you'll see *sedilia* (medieval stone niches used

ARTUR BOGACKI/SHUTTERSTOCK ©

as merchant stalls). The leader of the 1848–49 War of Independence, Lajos Kossuth, was held in a prison at No 9 from 1837 to 1840.

❹ Szentháromság tér

In the centre of I **Szentháromság tér** is a statue of the Holy Trinity, a 'plague pillar' first erected by grateful (and healthy) Buda citizens in the early 18th century. Across the square, the Hilton Budapest incorporates parts of a medieval Dominican church and a baroque Jesuit college.

❺ Former Ministry of Defence

Walking along Úri utca south to Dísz tér you'll come across the restored **former Ministry of Defence**, a casualty of WWII, and NATO's supposed nuclear target for Budapest during the Cold War. A long-overdue renovation has just been completed.

❻ Sándor Palace

Further south on the left is the restored **Sándor Palace** (Sándor palota), now housing the offices of the president of the republic. A rather low-key guard change takes place in front of the palace hourly between 9am and 5pm.

❼ Sikló

Between Sándor Palace and the Habsburg Steps leading to the Royal Palace is the upper station of the **Sikló** (p25), the funicular that will take you down to I Clark Ádám tér just west of the Chain Bridge.

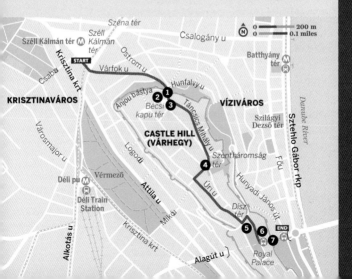

Best Walks
Erzsébetváros & the Jewish Quarter

This section of Erzsébetváros, stretching between the Big and Little Ring Rds, has always been predominantly Jewish, and this was the ghetto where Jews were forced to live behind wooden fences when the Nazis occupied Hungary in 1944. Walking through its streets is like stepping back in time.

Start VI Liszt Ferenc tér; Ⓜ Oktogon

Finish VII Dohány utca; Ⓜ Astoria

Length 1km; one to two hours

✕ Take a Break

Tel Aviv Cafe (☎06 30 438 7884; www.facebook.com/Cafe.Tel.Aviv.Budapest; VII Kazinczy utca 28; mains 1490-3400Ft; ⏰8am-8.30pm Sun-Thu, to 3pm Fri; 🚋4, 6), in the heart of the Jewish district, can oblige with Israeli-style kosher food – from couscous and shakshuka to hummus and pasta dishes (1390Ft to 2500Ft).

❶ Liszt Music Academy

Begin the walk in restaurant- and cafe-packed VI Liszt Ferenc tér, and poke your head into the sumptuous **Liszt Music Academy** (p100) at the southeastern end.

❷ Church of St Teresa

Walking southwest along Király utca you'll pass the **Church of St Teresa**, built in 1811 and containing a massive neoclassical altar designed by Mihály Pollack a decade later.

❸ Klauzál tér

Turning into Csányi utca, head southeast over Dob utca to the heart of the old Jewish Quarter, **Klauzál tér**. The square still has a feeling of pre-war Budapest. A continued Jewish presence is still evident in the surrounding streets, with several kosher restaurants, the wonderful **Fröhlich Cukrászda** cake shop and cafe, and a butcher just next to the **Orthodox Synagogue** (p101).

Liszt Music Academy

4 Ghetto Wall

Return to Dob utca, turn right on Holló utca and if the gate at Király utca 15 is open, walk to the rear of the courtyard to see a 30m-long piece of the original **ghetto wall** rebuilt in 2010. Votive lamps and stones stand before it in tribute to Holocaust victims.

5 Gozsdu udvar

The next turn on the left is the passageway called **Gozsdu udvar** (1901); now the district's number-one nightlife destination, and pulses with music and merry-makers come evening.

6 Carl Lutz Monument

At Dob utca 12 is an antifascist **monument to Carl Lutz**, a Swiss consul who, like Raoul Wallenberg, gave Jews false papers in 1944. It portrays an angel on high sending down a long cloth to a victim.

7 Murals

Around the corner, bordering a car park, are two large **murals**. The left one (2013) commemorates the 60th anniversary of the football victory of Hungary's 'Golden Team', the first time a continental team beat England at Wembley (6–3). The right one is an oversized Rubik's Cube, the difficult 3D puzzle invented in 1974 by Hungarian sculptor Ernő Rubik.

8 Great Synagogue

Retrace your steps and you'll find the **Great Synagogue** (p94) at the end of the street.

Best
Eating

The dining scene in Budapest has undergone a sea change in recent years. Hungarian food has 'lightened up', offering the same wonderfully earthy and spicy tastes but in less calorific dishes. The number of vegetarian restaurants has increased, and the choice of eateries with cuisines other than Magyar is greater than ever before.

Hungarian Cuisine

You might be familiar with some of the most common Hungarian dishes. *Gulyás* (goulash) is Hungary's signature dish, though here it's more like a soup than a stew and made with beef, onions and tomatoes. Paprika-infused *pörkölt* is closer to what we'd call goulash. *Halászlé* is a highly recommended fish soup made from poached freshwater fish, tomatoes, green peppers and paprika. *Savanyúság* (literally 'sourness') is anything from mildly sour-sweet cucumbers to almost acidic sauerkraut eaten with a main course. A popular dessert is *palacsinta,* a crêpe filled with jam, sweet cheese or chocolate sauce.

Types of Eateries

An *étterem* is a restaurant with a large selection, including international dishes. A *vendéglő* (or *kisvendéglő*) is smaller and usually serves inexpensive regional dishes or 'home cooking'. An *étkezde* or *kifőzde* is something like a diner, smaller and cheaper than *kisvendéglő* and often with counter seating. The overused term *csárda* originally signified a country inn with a rustic atmosphere, Gypsy music and hearty local dishes. Now any place that strings dried peppers on the wall and a couple of painted plates seems to call itself that. A *bisztró* is a much cheaper sit-down place that is often *önkiszolgáló* (self-service).

☑ Top Tips

▶ Eat your main meal at lunchtime; set meals at lunch at most restaurants – including high-end ones – cost a fraction of what they do at dinnertime.

▶ When tipping in a restaurant, never leave money on the table. Instead, tell waiters how much you intend to leave and they will give the change accordingly.

Best Local

Kéhli Vendéglő So famous that it appears in literature. (p57)

Kárpátia A fin-de-siècle stunner with Hungarian and Transylvanian specialities. (p68)

Fortuna Önkiszolgáló
Castle Hill's cheap and
cheery self-service
eatery. (p32)

Best Haute Cuisine

Borkonyha The 'Wine
Kitchen' is currently our
favourite in Pest, Michelin
accolades notwithstanding. (p81)

Csalogány 26 Haute
cuisine *à la hongroise* in
the heart of Buda. (p32)

Baraka Must-try fine dining in Belváros. (p69)

Best Modern Hungarian

Mák Inventive Hungarian dishes from a daily
changing blackboard.
(p82)

Fióka Buda Hills outpost
winning points for new-
style Hungarian dishes.
(p57)

Monk's Bistrot Industrial decor, daring ingredient pairings and great
lunch deals. (p68)

Laci! Konyha! Boutique
and very eclectic eatery
located in northern Pest.
(p89)

Best Traditional Hungarian

Kárpátia Serves mostly
meaty, expertly prepared,
modern Hungarian and
Transylvanian dishes.
(p68)

Kéhli Vendéglő Hungarian novelist Gyula Krúdy
was a fan of this rustic
restaurant. (p57)

Best Asian

Fuji Japán Budapest's
best Japanese restaurant, high in the Buda
Hills. (p57)

Oriental Soup House
Excellent *pho* and other

Vietnamese soups in
Northern Pest. (p89)

Best Italian

Da Mario Our new favourite Italian for superb
pasta dishes and wood-
fired pizzas. (p82)

Marcello This simple
Italian place has been a
student favourite for two
decades. (p44)

Best Jewish

Spinoza Café An amiable neighbourhood venue
that serves old favourites
and *klezmer* (Jewish folk
music). (p103)

Fröhlich Cukrászda
Kosher cake shop and
cafe in the former ghetto.
(p95)

Kőleves Jewish-inspired
(not kosher) menu with
good vegetarian choices.
(p102)

Best
Drinking

In recent years Budapest has justifiably gained a reputation as one of Europe's top nightlife destinations. Alongside its age-old cafe culture, it offers a magical blend of unique drinking holes, fantastic wine, home-grown fire waters and emerging craft beers, all served up with a warm Hungarian welcome and a wonderful sense of fun.

Pubs & Bars

Drinking establishments in the city run the gamut from quirky pubs and bohemian bars to much more refined wine and cocktail bars. If you want to sample the local beer (most commonly Dreher, Kőbányai and Arany Ászok) head for a *söröző*, a 'pub' with *csapolt sör* (draught beer) served in a *pohár* (0.3L glass) or *korsó* (0.4L or 0.5L glass). A *borozó* or *bor pince* is a traditional establishment (usually a dive) serving wine. Modern wine bars serve wine by the deci (decilitre, 0.1L) so you can sample a wide range.

Cafes

The *kávéház* (cafe) has long been an integral part of Budapest's social life and old-style cafes, some of which date back as much as a century and a half, abound in Budapest. The new breed of coffee house roasts its own blends and imports specific beans.

Ruin Pubs & Garden Clubs

Unique to Budapest, *romkocsmák* (ruin pubs) began to appear in the city in the early 2000s when abandoned buildings were turned into pop-up bars. At the same time, during the city's long and very hot summers, so-called *kertek* (literally 'gardens' but here any outdoor entertainment zone) empty out even the most popular indoor bars and clubs.

☑ Top Tips

▶ Pest's two main nightlife strips are trendy VI Liszt Ferenc tér, where you'll have to fight for a spot under the plane trees, and IX Ráday utca, a more subdued pedestrianised street in Józsefváros full of pubs, bars and modern cafes. Up and coming is V Szent István tér behind the basilica.

▶ www.wheretraveler.com/budapest is useful for nightlife listings.

Gerbeaud

Best Wine & Cocktail Bars

Doblo Romantic brick-lined bar with a huge variety of Hungarian wine. (p103)

Oscar American Bar Film decor and cool cocktails below the castle. (p34)

DiVino Borbár The place to taste your way through Hungary's wine regions. (p83)

Best Garden Clubs & Ruin Bars

Instant Multilevel venue with a bar for every taste. (p105)

Élesztő High-quality craft beer, and lots of it. (p117)

Best Coffee

Kávé Műhely This tiny Buda roastery serves great cakes, and stages vibrant contemporary art exhibitions. (p33)

Double Shot Grungy expat-founded, thimble-sized coffee shop in Újlipótváros, with excellent artisan coffee from around the globe. (p90)

Barako Kávéház Filipino-run coffee house that aims to spread the fame of Liberica Baraco coffee from the Philippines. (p57)

Best Traditional Cafes

Gerbeaud Dating back to 1858 and still serving impeccable cakes and coffee. (p65)

Lotz Terem Book Cafe Glamour, glitz and Károly Lotz frescoes at the back of a bookshop. (p104)

Centrál Kávéház Great for cakes, pastries and people-watching. (p70)

Ruszwurm Cukrászda Dating back to the early 19th century, this is the oldest traditional cafe in town. (p124)

Best Clubs

Corvin Club & Roof Terrace Rooftop dance floor with a view right across the city and quality DJs. (p117)

Gozsdu Manó Klub Cool cavern with an excellent sound system. (p105)

Best
Shopping

Budapest is a fantastic city for shopping, whether you're in the market for traditional folk craft with a twist, cutting-edge designer goods, the latest in flash headgear or honey-sweet dessert wine. Traditional markets stand side by side with mammoth shopping malls, and old-style umbrella makers can still be found next to avant-garde fashion boutiques.

Specialities & Souvenirs

Traditional items with a Hungarian branding – called Hungarica here – include folk embroidery and ceramics, pottery, wall hangings, painted wooden toys and boxes, dolls, all types of basketry, and porcelain (especially that from Herend and Zsolnay). Feather or goose-down pillows and duvets (comforters) are of exceptionally high quality.

Foodstuffs that are expensive or difficult to buy elsewhere – goose liver (both fresh and potted), dried mushrooms, jam (especially the apricot variety), prepared meats like Pick salami, the many types of paprika – make nice gifts (as long as you're allowed to take them into your country). Some of Hungary's 'boutique' wines also make excellent gifts; a bottle of six-*puttonyos* (the sweetest) Tokaji Aszú dessert wine always goes down a treat. *Pálinka* (fruit brandy) is a stronger option.

Markets

Some people consider a visit to one of Budapest's flea markets not just as a place to indulge their consumer vices, but also as the consummate Budapest experience. Make sure you visit one of the city's 20 large food markets, most of them in Pest. The vast majority are closed on Sunday, and Monday is always very quiet.

☑ Top Tips

▶ Antiques and art more than 50 years old require a permit from the Ministry of Culture for export; this involves a visit to a museum expert, photos of the piece and a National Bank form with proof-of-purchase receipts.

Best Gifts & Souvenirs

Le Parfum Croisette Hungary's only *parfumier*, with recipes going back 750 years. (p71)

Herend Contemporary and traditional fine porcelain – Hungary's answer to Wedgwood. (p34)

Best for Food & Drink

Bortársaság The first port of call for buying wine. (p34)

Mézes Kuckó Still the very best place in town for nut-and-honey cookies. (p91)

Rózsavölgyi Csokoládé Artisan chocolate bars and bonbons, beautifully packaged. (p71)

Best for Fashion & Clothing

Printa Locally designed bags, leather goods and T-shirts. (p106)

Vass Shoes Classic footwear – cobbled for you or ready to wear. (p71)

Best for Books

Bestsellers Budapest's most complete English-language bookshop; helpful staff. (p83)

Massolit Budapest New and secondhand in an atmospheric old shop with a little garden. (p106)

Múzeum Antikvárium Used and antique books opposite the Hungarian National Museum. (p113)

Best for Antiques

BÁV Check out any branch of this pawn and secondhand shop chain if you can't make it to the flea markets. (p83)

Pintér Galéria Over 2000 sq metres of antiques. (p83)

Best Markets

Nagycsarnok Huge market hall selling everything from fruit and veg to paprika and goose liver. (p112)

Rákóczi tér market Authentic local market with products fresh from the farm. (p113)

Gouba Weekly arts and crafts market in the heart of Erzsébetváros. (p106)

 Worth a Trip

One of the biggest flea markets in Central Europe, **Ecseri Piac** (www.piaconline.hu; XIX Nagykőrösi út 156; ⊙8am-4pm Mon-Fri, 5am-3pm Sat, 8am-1pm Sun) sells everything from antique jewellery and Soviet army watches to top hats. Early Saturday is the best day to go. Take bus 54 from Pest's Boráros tér, or for a quicker journey, express bus 84E, 89E or 94E from the Határ út stop on the M3 metro line in Pest and get off at the Fiume utca stop.

Best
Entertainment

For a city of its size, Budapest has a huge choice of things to do and places to go after dark – from opera and folk dancing to live jazz and films screened in palatial cinemas. It's usually not difficult getting tickets or getting in; the hard part is deciding what to do and where to go.

Best Classical Music

Liszt Music Academy Budapest's premier venue for classical concerts is also an art nouveau treasure house. (p100)

Palace of Arts The city's most up-to-date cultural venue with two concert halls and near-perfect acoustics. (p117)

Hungarian State Opera House Small but perfectly formed home to both the state opera company and the Hungarian National Ballet. (p80)

Best Live Music

Spinoza Café An excellent place to see *klezmer* (Jewish folk music) concerts. (p103)

Akvárium Klub In an old bus terminal, two large halls serve up a quality line-up of live acts. (p70)

Gödör Great gigs in the midst of banging Erzsébetváros. (p105)

A38 Watertight watering hole on the water (it's a ship) voted the world's best. (p46)

Best Jazz & Blues

Budapest Jazz Club Reliable music venue still swings in its new location. (p91)

Jedermann Relaxed Ráday utca hang-out for jazz and great grills. (p113)

☑ **Top Tips**

▶ Useful freebies for popular listings include *Budapest Funzine* (www.funzine.hu) and *PestiEst* (www.est.hu) and, for more serious offerings, the Koncert Kalendárium website (www.muzsikalendarium.hu).

▶ Handy websites for booking theatre and concert tickets include www.kulturinfo.hu and www.jegymester.hu.

▶ www.ticket.info.hu is a good place to make bookings for concerts and cruises.

Best
With Kids

Budapest abounds in places that will delight children, and there is always a special child's entry rate (and often a family one as well) to paying attractions. Visits to many areas of the city can be designed around a rest stop or picnic – at City Park, say, or on Margaret Island.

STEFAN CIOATA/GETTY IMAGES ©

Best Museums & Galleries

Museum of Fine Arts Program allows kids to handle original Egyptian artefacts and create their own works of art. (p119)

Aquincum Museum Great interactive exhibits, including virtual duelling with a gladiator. (p59)

Vasarely Museum Might be adult themed, but the wacky art – which seems to move about the canvas of its own accord – will surprise and please kids of all ages. (p54)

Best Entertainment

Budapest Puppet Theatre Kids will be transfixed by the marionette shows if they

don't speak Hungarian. (p106)

Budapest Zoo World-class collection of big cats, hippopotamuses, polar bears and giraffes. (p121)

Gellért Baths An abundance of outdoor and indoor pools; the outdoor one has a wave machine. (p38)

Best Public Transport

Sikló Climbing up to Castle Hill at an angle. (p25)

Cog Railway This unusual conveyance will delight kids. (p61)

Children's Railway Kids in charge in the Buda Hills. (p61)

☑ Top Tips

▶ Most restaurants won't have a set children's menu but will split the adult portion. When they do they're usually priced around 1200Ft.

▶ Budapest's traditional cafes and *cukrászdák* (cake shops) will satisfy a sweet tooth of any size.

▶ A cafe made for kids is **Briós** (☎1-789 6110; www.brioskavezo. hu; XIII Pozsonyi út 16; ⊙7.30am-10pm; ☐trolleybus 75, 76) in Újlipótváros.

Best
Architecture

Budapest's architectural waltz through history begins with the Romans at Aquincum, moves up to Castle Hill's medieval streets, over to the ruins of Margaret Island and into the many splendid baroque churches on either side of the Danube. Neoclassicism chips in with the Basilica of St Stephen and the Hungarian National Museum. But the capital really hits its stride with its art nouveau masterpieces.

Best Roman

Aquincum A 2nd-century paved street and outlines of houses and public buildings in Óbuda. (p58)

Best Medieval

Castle Museum Highlights include the Gothic Hall, Royal Cellar and 14th-century Tower Chapel. (p27)

Margaret Island Remains of an early Franciscan church and monastery and a Dominican convent.

Best Turkish Era

Rudas Baths Octagonal pool, domed cupola and massive columns from the 16th century. (p44)

Gül Baba's Tomb Mosque and last resting place of 16th-century dervish. (p54)

Király Baths Another great structure dating from Turkish times, with a wonderful skylit central dome. (p31)

Best Baroque

Holy Trinity Statue Stunning example of ecclesiastical baroque on Castle Hill.

Citadella The best example of civic (or secular) baroque in Budapest. (p40)

Best Neoclassical

Hungarian National Museum Textbook example of this style from the late 1840s. (p110)

Basilica of St Stephen The dome is the giveaway of this neoclassical delight that took 50 years to build. (p76)

Best Art Nouveau

Museum of Applied Arts Zsolnay roof tiles, central marble hall and 'Moghul' turrets and domes. (p115)

Philanthia Probably the most complete art nouveau interior in Budapest. (p65)

Best
Gay & Lesbian

Budapest offers just a reasonable gay scene for its size. Most gay people are discreet in public places and displays of affection are rare. Lesbian social life remains very much underground, with a lot of private parties. There have been a couple of violent right-wing demonstrations in response to the Budapest Pride celebrations in the recent past. Attitudes are changing, but society generally remains conservative on this issue. Budapest was also the venue for EuroGames 2012 – Europe's largest gay-friendly sporting event.

NP/SHUTTERSTOCK ©

Best Gay & Lesbian Venues

Alterego Still the city's premier gay club (and don't you forget it). (p83)

CoXx Men's Bar Three bars and a whole world of cruising. (p105)

Best Gay- & Lesbian-Friendly Accommodation

Casati Budapest Hotel Tasteful conversion in the centre of Pest with cool decor and funky covered courtyard. (p147)

☑ Top Tips

▸ **Budapest GayGuide** (www.budapest.gayguide.net) Good listings and insider advice.

▸ **Gay Budapest** (www.budapest-gay.com) Of some use for accommodation.

▸ **Háttér Society** (☎ 1-329 2670; www.hatter.hu; open 6pm to 11pm) Advice and help line.

▸ **Labrisz** (www.labrisz.hu) Info on the city's lesbian scene.

▸ **Radio Pink** (www.radiopink.hu) Hungary's gay radio, broadcast through web-based live stream.

Best
Tours

Best Walking Tours

Walking tours are run by various companies and most tend to be standard three-hour jaunts that take in the city's main attractions.

Free Budapest Tours (📞06 70 424 0569; www.freebudapesttours.eu; V Deák Ferenc tér; admission free; 🕐10.30am & 2.30pm) A 2½-hour tour of both Pest and Buda leaves from V Deák Ferenc tér (opposite Le Meridien Hotel) daily at 10.30am, and the 1½-hour tour of Pest leaves from the same place at 2.30pm. Guides work for tips only, so dig deep into your pockets.

Absolute Walking Tours (📞1-269 3843; www.absolute-tours.com; VI Lázár utca 16, Absolute Tours Centre; adult/student/child €34/32/17; 🕐10am year-round, plus 2.30pm Mon, Wed, Fri & Sat Apr-Oct; Ⓜ M1 Opera) A 3½-hour guided walk through City Park, central Pest and Castle Hill run by the people behind Yellow Zebra Bikes. Tours depart daily from the Absolute Tours Centre behind the Opera House. Also offers several specialist tours, including the popular 3½-hour Hammer & Sickle Tour (adult/student/child €54/50/27) of Budapest's communist past.

Best Bus Tours

Hugely popular are hop-on, hop-off bus tours that allow you to board and alight as you please for a selected length of time.

Program Centrum (📞1-317 7767; www.programcentrum.hu; V Erzsébet tér 9-11, Le Meridien Hotel; adult/0-8yr €22/free; Ⓜ M1/2/3 Deák Ferenc tér, 🚌47, 49) Valid on two bus routes (one taped in 24 languages, one live commentary in English and German) and a one-hour river cruise for 48 hours.

Cityrama (📞1-302 4382; www.cityrama.hu; V Báthory utca 22; adult/concession 8500/4250Ft; 🚌15, 115, Ⓜ M3 Arany

☑ **Top Tips**

▶ The **Budapest Card** includes two free guided tours and offers discounts on other organised tours.

János utca) If you prefer to stay on the bus, this operator offers three-hour city tours, with several photo stops and live commentary in five languages.

Best Cycling Tours

Most bike-hire companies offer tours for around 5000Ft to 5500Ft per person, but itineraries often depend on the whim of the group leader.

Yellow Zebra Bikes (📞1-269 3843; www.yellowzebra-bikes.com; VI Lázár utca 16;

tours adult/student/3-12yr €28/26/12; ☉9am-8.30pm Apr-Oct, to 7pm Nov-Mar; Ⓜ M1 Opera) Tours take in Heroes' Sq, City Park, central Pest and Castle Hill in around four hours and include the bike. Depart from in front of the Discover Budapest office behind the Opera House at 11am daily from April to October (also at 5pm July and August). In winter departures are at 11am on Friday, Saturday and Sunday only.

Best Boat Tours

A slew of companies offer cruises on the Danube that include taped commentary in a multitude of languages and (usually) a free drink.

Mahart PassNave
(☎1-484 4013; www. mahartpassnave.hu; V Belgrád rakpart, Vidadó tér Pier; adult/student/ child 2990/2490/1490Ft; ☉10am-9pm late Mar–late Oct, to 10pm Jul & Aug; ⛴2) One-hour trip between Margaret and Rákóczi Bridges departs hourly.

Legenda (☎1-266 4190; www.legenda. hu; V Vigadó tér, pier 7; adult/student/child day 3900/3500/2400Ft, night 5500/4400/2750Ft; ⛴2) Similar deal in 30 languages has between five and six daily departures but only in winter.

River Ride (☎1-332 2555; www.riverride.com; V Széchenyi István tér 7-8; adult/child 8500/6000Ft; ⛴2) Amphibious bus takes you on a two-hour heart-stopping tour of Budapest by road and river; live commentary (English and German).

Best Special-Interest Tours

A number of local tour companies run specialised city tours. Some combine driving and walking, while others are strictly walking tours; themes include Jewish history, contemporary art, art nouveau, Budapest's nightlife and more.

Jewish Heritage Tours (☎1-317 1377; www.ticket.

info.hu; Deák Ferenc tér; Ⓜ M1/2/3 Deák Ferenc tér, ⛴47, 49) Recommended tours delve into the culture and history of Budapest's Jewish community. The Essential Tour (adult/ student 6900/6500Ft, 2½ hours) takes in the two most important synagogues, as well as the streets of the Jewish Quarter, while the Grand Tour (11,400/10,400Ft, 3½ to 4 hours) includes all the stops of the Essential Tour, as well as Raoul Wallenberg Memorial Park, Godzsu udvar and a third synagogue.

Budapest Underguide (☎06 30 908 1597; www. underguide.com; Sas utca 15; per person from 9250Ft; Ⓜ M1 Bajcsy-Zsilinszky út) This outfit gets rave reviews from visitors for its themed private four-hour tours. Themes include fashion and design, art nouveau, communism, Budapest's best bars, contemporary art and Buda Castle for children.

Best
Thermal Baths & Pools

Budapest lies on the geological fault separating the Buda Hills from the Great Plain, and more than 30,000 cu metres of warm to scalding (21°C to 76°C) mineral water gush forth daily from some 123 thermal and more than 400 mineral springs. As a result, the city is a major spa centre and 'taking the waters' at one of the city's many baths, be they Turkish time warps, art nouveau marvels or modern establishments, is a real Budapest experience.

What's Inside

The layout of most of Budapest's baths – both old and new – follows a similar pattern: a series of indoor thermal pools, where temperatures range from warm to hot, with steam rooms, saunas, ice-cold plunge pools and rooms for massage. Some have outdoor pools with fountains, wave machines and whirlpools.

Most baths offer a full range of serious medical treatments plus more indulgent services such as massage (5500/7500Ft for 20/30 minutes) and pedicure (4500Ft). Specify what you want when buying your ticket.

Depending on the time and day, a few baths can be for men or women only. There are usually mixed days and nowadays most baths – including the **Széchenyi**, **Gellért** and **Király Baths** – are always for men and women together. On single-sex days or in same-sex sections, men are usually handed drawstring loincloths and women apron-like garments to wear, though the use of bathing suits is on the increase even on single-sex days. You must wear a bathing suit on mixed-sex days; these are

☑ **Top Tips**

▶ Opening times and whether everybody/men/women are welcome depend on the day of the week, but most baths are now completely mixed. Many open on weekend nights.

▶ Admission starts at 2400Ft; in theory this allows you to stay for 1½/two hours on weekends/weekdays, though this is seldom enforced nowadays.

▶ Budapest Spas and Hot Springs (www.spasbudapest. com) has excellent and up-to-date information.

Gellért Baths (p38)

available for hire (1350Ft to 2000Ft) if you don't have your own.

Getting In & Out

The procedure for getting out of your street clothes and into the water requires some explanation. All baths and pools have cabins or lockers. In most of the baths nowadays you are given an electronic bracelet that directs you to, and then opens, your locker or cabin. Ask for assistance if you can't work it out. The method used in the past was a bit more complicated: you would find a free locker or cabin yourself and – after you got

Széchenyi Baths (p119)

Art nouveau architecture at Gellért Baths (p38)

changed in (or beside) it – you would call the attendant, who would lock it for you and hand you a numbered tag. You had to remember your locker number; in a bid to prevent thefts the number on the tag was not the same as the one on the locker.

What to Bring

Though some of the baths look a little rough around the edges, they are clean and the water is changed regularly. However, you might consider taking along a pair of plastic sandals or flip-flops/thongs.

Many places require the use of a bathing cap; bring your own or wear the disposable ones provided or sold for 700Ft.

Bring a towel, otherwise most pools have them for rent (1000Ft).

Choosing a Bath

Rudas Baths These renovated baths are the most Turkish of all in Budapest, built in 1566, with an octagonal pool, domed cupola with coloured glass and eight massive pillars. They're mostly men-only during the week but turn into a real zoo on mixed weekend nights. (p44)

Gellért Baths Soaking in these art nouveau baths, now open to both men and women at all times, has been likened to taking a bath in a cathedral. The indoor swimming pools are the most beautiful in the city. (p38)

Széchenyi Baths The gigantic 'wedding-cake' building in City Park houses the Széchenyi Baths, which are unusual for three reasons: their immensity (a dozen thermal baths and three outdoor swimming pools); the bright, clean atmosphere; and the high temperature of the water (up to 40°C). (p119)

Veli Bej Baths This venerable (1575) Turkish bath in Buda has got a new lease of life after having been forgotten for centuries. (p54)

Király Baths The four small Turkish pools here, while begging for renovation, are the real McCoy and date back to 1570. (p31)

Best
Museums & Galleries

Unlike most other European cities, Budapest does not have a single museum founded from a royal treasury. Instead, support came from an increasingly politicised aristocracy, which saw the value of safeguarding the nation's relics and artwork. Today the city counts some five dozen museums devoted to subjects as diverse as op art, musical instruments, trade and tourism, and folk costume.

Best History Museums

Aquincum Museum Excellent purpose-built museum with large collection of Roman finds. (p59)

Castle Museum Renovated museum walks you through Budapest history painlessly. (p27)

Best Art Museums

Vasarely Museum Devoted to op art – and still as wacky and mesmerising as ever. (p54)

Hungarian National Gallery Treasure house of the most important Hungarian artwork. (p25)

Museum of Applied Arts Come for the sumptuous interior

and vast collection of art nouveau furniture. (p115)

Best Cultural Museums

Memento Park Last resting place of Communist-era statues and monuments. (p48)

Music History Museum Filled with scores and musical instruments that play. (p30)

Hungarian Museum of Trade & Tourism The catering and hospitality trade through objects and advertising. (p55)

Hungarian Jewish Museum The story of Hungarian Jewry from the time of the Romans until the Holocaust. (p95)

INAXANHATEREN/SHUTTERSTOCK ©

☑ Top Tips

▶ Wear comfortable shoes and make use of the cloakrooms.

▶ Choose a particular period or section and pretend that the rest of the museum is somewhere across town.

▶ The Museum of Fine Arts (p119) is due to reopen in 2018 after three years' extensive renovation. Artwork from the mid-19th century onwards is due to relocate to the yet-to-be-built Hungarian National Gallery–Ludwig Museum in City Park.

Best
Parks & Gardens

Budapest and vicinity counts some eight protected landscape areas and more than 30 nature conservation areas. The largest area within the city proper encompasses the Buda Hills, the lungs of the city and a 105-sq-km protected area of steep ravines, rocky grasslands and more than 150 caves. Less 'wild' green spaces can be found through the city on both sides of the Danube.

City Park Enormous City Park is filled with (mostly paid) attractions, but entry to the park is free. (p118)

Japanese Garden Margaret Island is replete with gardens, most notably the Japanese Garden at the northern end. (p90)

Buda Hills A magnet for hikers, the Buda Hills also contain a number of nature reserves. (p60)

Budapest Zoo Not just a menagerie but a botanical garden too, with a Japanese Garden and Palm House. (p121)

Károly Garden The oldest public garden in the city is hidden deep in the Inner Town. (p70)

Szabadság tér The gardens in this huge square are often overlooked in favour of the grandiose buildings around it. (p81)

Castle Garden Bazaar Newly reopened and renovated pleasure park (dating from 1893) in Tabán. (p44)

☑ **Top Tips**

▶ The best time to take a walk in Budapest's parks is in mid- or late spring when the flowers and trees are in full blossom. These green places also provide shade from the scorching summer heat. A walk in a park between mid-September and mid-October will reward with beautiful foliage, though winter is often rather bleak.

Survival Guide

Survival Guide

Before You Go

When to Go

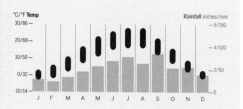

°C/°F Temp
30/86 —
20/68 —
10/50 —
0/32 —
-10/14 —

Rainfall inches/mm
— 6/150
— 4/100
— 2/50
— 0

J F M A M J J A S O N D

Spring (Apr–Jun) Often wet, but just glorious, with fewer tourists.

Summer (Jul & Aug) Warm, sunny and unusually long. Expect higher prices and long queues.

Autumn (Sep & Oct) Beautiful, particularly in the Buda Hills; festivals mark the *szüret* (grape harvest).

Winter (Nov–Mar) Can be cold and bleak; some attractions curtail their hours or shut entirely till mid-March.

Book Your Stay

➡ In general, accommodation is more limited in the Buda neighbourhoods than on the other side of the Danube River in Pest

➡ A cheap hotel is generally more expensive than private room, but may be the answer if you are only staying one night or arrive too late to get a room through an agency.

➡ Hotels – *szállók* or *szállodák* in Hungarian – can be anything from (rapidly disappearing) run-down socialist-era brutalist constructions to luxurious five-star palaces and quirky boutique and design hotels.

➡ Because of the changing value of the forint, many midrange and top-end hotels quote their rates in euros, as we have here.

eful Websites

Discover Budapest
ww.discoverbudapest.
m) Tour company that
so books accommoda-
n.

**Hungarian Tourism
C** (www.gotohungary.
m) Top-heavy with ac-
mmodation choices in
e capital.

Lonely Planet (www.
nelyplanet.com/
dapest/hotels)
commendations and
okings.

Mellow Mood Group
ww.mellowmood.hu)
nain with a big variety of
tions.

Best Hotel Service
ww.besthotelservice.
) Good for budget ac-
mmodation.

Hip Homes Hungary
ww.hiphomeshungary.
m) Fabulous short-
rm apartments.

est Budget

averick City Lodge
ww.maverick
dges.com) Modern,
arehouse-style hostel
th great facilities.

antee House (www.
ckpackbudapest.hu)
udapest's first hostel
ows (up) in size and
esign.

Groove (www.groove
hostel.hu) Individually
decorated, cavernous
dorms, oodles of
backpacker perks and a
friendly vibe.

Zen House (www.
zenhouse-budapest.com)
Peaceful, family-run place
awash with Buddha im-
ages and plants, offering
spacious, stylish private
rooms.

Best Midrange

Baltazár (www.baltazar
budapest.com) Midrange
hotel with a high-end
Castle location.

**Casati Budapest
Hotel** (www.casatibuda-
pesthotel.com) An artful
conversion of a beautiful
building with sustainable
credentials.

Budapest Rooms (www.
budapestrooms.eu) Well-
run, good-looking B&B
and a very helpful host.

Hotel Papillon (www.
hotelpapillon.hu) Delightful 'country-style' hotel in
the Buda Hills.

Best Top End

Buddha Bar Hotel
(www.buddhabarhotel
budapest.com) Opulent

makeover of one of the
towering Klotild Palaces.

Art'otel Budapest (www.
artotels.com/budapest)
Uber-designed caravan-
serai hard by the Danube.

**Kempinski Hotel
Corvinus** (www.
kempinski-budapest.
com) Probably the best-
run hotel in town.

Hotel Palazzo Zichy
(www.hotel-palazzozichy.
hu) Impressive palace
hotel on a lovely little
square.

Arriving in Budapest

Ferenc Liszt International Airport

Budapest's **Ferenc Liszt
International Airport**
(BUD; ☎1-296 7000; www.
bud.hu) has two modern
terminals side by side,
24km southeast of the
city centre.

Terminal 2A deals
with departures and
arrivals from Schengen
countries. Flights to and
from non-Schengen

destinations use Terminal 2B, which is next door. The new SkyCourt connects the two terminals.

At both terminals and in the SkyCourt you'll find currency-exchange desks operated by **Interchange** (⏰8am-1am) and ATMs. In Terminal 2A there are half a dozen car-hire desks. Luggage lockers are available around the clock on the ground floor of the SkyCourt.

Bus & Metro The cheapest (and most time-consuming) way to get into the city centre from the airport is to take bus 200E (350Ft, on the bus 450Ft; 4am to midnight) – look for the stop on the footpath between terminals 2A and 2B – which terminates at the Kőbánya-Kispest metro station. From there take the M3 metro into the city centre. The total cost is 700Ft to 800Ft. Between midnight and 4am night bus 900 makes the run.

Shuttle The **MiniBUD** (📞1-550 0000; www.minibud.hu; one way from 1900Ft) airport shuttle carries passengers from both terminals directly to their hotel, hostel or residence in nine-seat vans. Tickets are available at a clearly marked desk in the arrivals halls, though you may have to wait while the van fills up. You need to book your journey back to the airport at least 12 hours in advance.

Taxi Reputable **Fő Taxi** (📞1-222 2222; www.fotaxi.hu) has the monopoly on picking up passengers at the airport. Fares to most locations in Pest are about 6000Ft, and in Buda about 7000Ft.

Keleti, Nyugati & Déli Train Stations

➡ All three train stations are on metro lines of the same name; Keleti is on the green M4 and the blue M3; Nyugati is on the M3; Déli on the red M2.

➡ Night buses serve all three stations when the metro is closed.

➡ Left-luggage lockers are available at all stations.

Stadion & Népliget Bus Stations

➡ Stadion is on the red metro M2; Népliget is on the blue metro M3.

➡ All international buses arrive and depart from Népliget.

➡ Stadion generally serves cities and towns eastern Hungary.

International Ferry Pier

➡ Hydrofoils arrive at and depart from the International Ferry Pier which is between Elizabeth and Liberty Bridges on the Pest side. It's on tram line 2 and close to the Fővám tér station of the M4 metro line.

➡ **Mahart PassNave** (📞1-484 4013; www.mahartpassnave.hu; V Belgrád rakpart, Vidadó tér Pier; adult/student/child 2990/2490/1490Ft; ⏰10am-9pm late Mar–late Oct, to 10pm Jul & Aug; 🚢2) runs daily hydrofoil services on the Danube River between Budapest and Vienna (5½ to 6½ hours) from mid-May to late September.

Getting Around

Metro

Budapest has four underground metro lines. Three of them converge at Deák Ferenc tér (only): the little yellow (or Millennium) line designated M1 that runs from Vörösmarty tér to Mexikói út in Pest; the red M2 line from Déli train station in Buda to Örs vezér tere in Pest; and the blue M3 line from Újpest-Központ to Kőbánya-Kispest in Pest. The green M4 metro runs from Kelenföld train station in southern Buda to Keleti train station in Pest, where it links with the M2. It links with the M3 at Kálvin tér.

All four metro lines run from about 4am and begin their last journey at around 11.15pm.

The basic fare for all forms of transport is a 350Ft ticket (3000Ft for a block of 10).

Tickets have to be validated in machines at metro entrances and on board other vehicles – inspectors will fine you for not doing so.

Bus

➡ Extensive system of buses running on 260 routes day and night from around 4.15am to between 9pm and 11.30pm.

➡ From 11.30pm to just after 4am a network of 41 night buses (indicated by three digits and beginning with '9') operates every 15 to 60 minutes, depending on the route.

Tram

➡ A network of 30 lines; often faster and more pleasant for sightseeing than buses.

➡ Tram 6 runs every 10 to 15 minutes around the clock, including overnight.

Taxi

➡ Cheap by European standards, with uniform flag-fall (450Ft) and per-kilometre charges (280Ft).

➡ Never get into a taxi that does not have a yellow licence plate and an identification badge displayed on the dashboard (as required by law), plus the logo of one of the reputable taxi firms on the outside of the side doors and a table of fares clearly visible on the right-side back door.

➡ Reputable operators include **Budapest Taxi** (☏ 1-777 7777; www. budapesttaxi.hu), **City Taxi** (☏ 1-211 1111; www.citytaxi. hu), **Fő Taxi** (☏ 1-222 2222; www.fotaxi.hu) and **Taxi 4** (☏ 1-444 4444; www. taxi4.hu).

Essential Information

Discount Cards

Budapest Card (% 1-438 8080; www.budapestinfo. hu; per 24/27/72 hours 4655/7505/9405Ft) Free entry to selected museums and sights in and around the city; unlimited travel on all forms of public transport; two free guided walking tours; and discounts for organised tours, car rental, thermal baths, and at selected shops and restaurants. Available at tourist offices but cheaper online.

Electricity

Type F
230V/50Hz

Emergency & Important Numbers

Any crime must be reported at the police station of the district you are in. In the centre of Pest this is the **Belváros-Lipótváros Police Station** (📞1-373 1000; V Szalay utca 11-13; Ⓜ M2 Kossuth Lajos tér). If possible, bring along a Hungarian speaker.

General Emergency (📞112)

Ambulance (📞 104; in English 📞 1-311 1666)

Police (📞 107)

Fire (📞 105)

Internet Access

➡ Wireless (wi-fi) access is available at most hostels/hotels; few charge for the service. Many restaurants, cafes and bars offer wi-fi, usually free to paying customers.

➡ Some hostels and hotels have at least one computer available to guests either free or for a small sum. Internet cafes are rapidly disappearing due to the proliferation of smartphones and wi-fi.

Money

Currency Hungary's currency is the forint (Ft). Many hotels state prices in euros.

ATMs Everywhere.

Credit Cards Widely accepted everywhere.

Changing Money Avoid moneychangers (especially those on V Váci utca) in favour of banks.

Tipping Widely practised. In restaurants, for decent service tip 10–15%; never leave money on the table, instead, tell waiters how much you intend to leave

and they will give the change accordingly. For taxis, you can round up the fare.

Opening Hours

➡ Businesses almost always post opening hours on their door. *Nyitva* means 'open', *zárva* 'closed'.

➡ In summer, some sho close early on Fri and shut down altogether fo at least part of August.

Banks 7.45am to 5pm Mon to Thu, to 4pm Fri

Bars 11am to midnight Sun to Thu, to 2am Fri and Sat

Clubs 4pm to 2am Sun Thu, to 4am Fri and Sat; some weekends only

Grocery stores and su permarkets 7am to 7pr Mon to Fri, to 3pm Sat; some also to noon Sun

Restaurants 11am to 11pm; breakfast venues open by 8am

Shops 10am to 6pm Mc to Fri, to 1pm Sat

Public Holidays

New Year's Day 1 Janua

National Day 15 March

ster Monday
arch/April

bour Day 1 May

hit Monday May/June

Stephen's Day
August

56 Remembrance
y/Republic Day
October

Saints' Day
ovember

ristmas holidays 25 &
December

afe Travel

Don't even think of
ling 'black' (without
ying a fare) on public
ansport – you will be
ught and severely
ed.

Pickpocketing is quite
mmon in public places.

Excessive billing of cus-
mers still occasionally
ppens in some bars
d restaurants, so check
ur bill carefully.

elephone

For local calls, dial the
mber (seven digits in
udapest, six elsewhere).

All localities in
ungary have a two-
git area code, except

for Budapest, which has
just a ☑1.

➡ You must always dial
☑06 when ringing
mobile phones, which
have specific area
codes depending on the
company.

Tourist Information

➡ **Budapest Info** (Map
p120; ☑1-438 8080; www.
budapestinfo.hu; V Sütő utca
2; ☺8am-8pm; Ⓜ M1/2/3
Deák Ferenc tér) is the
main tourist office; there
is another **branch** (Map
Olof Palme sétány 5, City Ice
Rink; ☺9am-7pm; Ⓜ M1
Hősök tere) in City Park
and info desks in the
arrivals sections of Fer-
enc Liszt International
Airport's Terminals 2A
and 2B.

➡ www.xpatloop.com is a
handy source of info by
the city's extensive expat
community.

➡ www.spasbudapest.
com gives you the low-
down on the city's spas.

Travellers with Disabilities

➡ Budapest has taken
great strides in recent
years in making public

areas and facilities
more accessible to the
disabled. Wheelchair
ramps, toilets fitted for
those with disabilities
and inward-opening
doors, though not as
common as in Western
Europe, do exist. Audible
traffic signals for the
blind are becoming com-
monplace, as are Braille
plates in public lifts.

➡ Download Lonely Plan-
et's free Accessible Travel
guide from http://lptravel.
to/AccessibleTravel.

➡ Contact the **Hungarian**
Federation of Disabled
Persons' Associations
(MEOSZ; Map p52, C1; ☑1-
388 2387; www.meoszinfo.
hu; III San Marco utca 76;
☺8am-4pm Mon-Fri) for
more info.

Visas

➡ Citizens of all Euro-
pean countries and of
Australia, Canada, Israel,
Japan, New Zealand and
the USA do not require
visas for visits of up to
90 days.

➡ Check current visa
requirements on the
website of the **Minis-**
try of Foreign Affairs
(www.konzuliszolgalat.
kormany.hu).

Language

Hungarian is a member of the Finno-Ugric language family; it is related very distantly to Finnish and Estonian. There are approximately 14.5 million speakers of Hungarian.

Hungarian has polite and informal forms; when addressing people you don't know well, use the polite form. In this language guide, polite forms are used.

To enhance your trip with a phrasebook, visit **lonelyplanet.com**.

Basics

Hello. (singular/plural)
Szervusz.	*ser·vus*
Szervusztok.	*ser·vus·tawk*

Goodbye.
Viszont-	*vi·sawnt·*
látásra	*laa·taash·ro*

Yes./No.
Igen./Nem.	*i·gen/nem*

Please. (pol/inf)
Kérem.	*kay·rem*

Thank you.
Köszönöm.	*keu·seu·neum*

You're welcome.
Szívesen.	*see·ve·shen*

Excuse me.
Elnézést	*el·nay·zaysht*
kérek.	*kay·rek*

Sorry.
Sajnálom.	*shoy·naa·lawm*

How are you?
Hogy van	*hawd' von*

Fine. And you?
Jól. És Ön?	*yāwl aysh eun*

Do you speak English?
Beszél angolul?	*be·sayl on·gaw·lul*

I don't understand.
Nem értem.	*nem ayr·tem*

Eating & Drinking

The menu, please.
Az étlapot,	*az ayt·lo·pawt*
kérem.	*kay·rem*

I'd like a local speciality.
Valamilyen helyi	*vo·lo·mi·yen he·yi*
specialitást	*shpe·tsi·o·li·taasht*
szeretnék.	*se·ret·nayk*

What would you recommend?
Mit ajánlana?	*mit o·yaan·lo·no*

Do you have vegetarian food?
Vannak önöknél	*von·nok*
vegetáriánus	*eu·neuk·nayl*
ételek?	*ve·ge·taa·ri·aa·nus*
	ay·te·lek

I'd like..., please.
Legyen szíves,	*le·dyen see·vesh*
hozzon egy...	*hawz·zawn ej...*

Cheers! (to one person)
Egészségére!	*e·gays·shay·gay·re*

Cheers! (to more than one person)
Egészségükre!	*e·gays·shay·gewk·re*

That was delicious!
Ez nagyon	*ez no·dyawn*
finom volt!	*fi·nawm vawlt*

Please bring the bill.
Kérem, hozza a	*kay·rem hawz·zo o*
számlát.	*saam·laat*

Shopping

I want to buy ...
Szeretnék venni ...	*se·ret·nayk ven·ni ...*

I'm just looking.
Csak nézegetek.	*chok nay·ze·ge·tek*

n I look at it?
egnézhetem?   *meg·nayz·he·tem*

w much is this?
ennyibe kerül   *men'·yi·be ke·rewl*
?   *ez*

at's too expensive.
 túl drága.   *ez tūl draa·go*

ere's a mistake in the bill.
lami hiba van a   *vo·lo·mi hi·bo von o*
ámlában.   *saam·laa·bon*

mergencies

lp!
gítség!   *she·geet·shayg*

 away!
enjen el!   *men·yen el*

ll the police!
vja a   *heev·yo o*
ndőrséget!   *rend·ēūr·shay·get*

ll a doctor!
vjon   *heev·yawn*
vost!   *awr·vawsht*

 lost.
évedtem.   *el·tay·ved·tem*

 sick.
sszul vagyok.   *raws·sul vo·dyawk*

ere are the toilets?
l a véce?   *hawl o vay·tse*

me & Numbers

at time is it?
ny óra?   *haan' āw·ra*

s (one/10) o'clock.
gy/Tíz) óra van.   *(ed'/teez) āw·ra von*

orning	*reggel*	*reg·gel*
ernoon	*délután*	*dayl·u·taan*
ening	*este*	*esh·te*

sterday	*tegnap*	*teg·nop*
day	*ma*	*mo*
morrow	*holnap*	*hawl·nop*

1	*egy*	*ed'*
2	*kettő*	*ket·tēū*
3	*három*	*haa·rawm*
4	*négy*	*nayd'*
5	*öt*	*eut*
6	*hat*	*hot*
7	*hét*	*hayt*
8	*nyolc*	*nyawlts*
9	*kilenc*	*ki·lents*
10	*tíz*	*teez*
100	*száz*	*saaz*
1000	*ezer*	*e·zer*

Transport & Directions

Where's (the market)?
Hol van (a piac)?   *hawl von (o pi·ots)*

What's the address?
Mi a cím?   *mi o tseem*

Can you show me (on the map)?
Meg tudja   *meg tud·yo*
mutatni   *mu·tot·ni*
nekem (a   *ne·kem (o*
térképen)?   *tayr·kay·pen)*

Does it stop at (Parliament)?
Megáll   *meg·aall*
(Parlamenthez)   *(por·lo·ment·hez)*
on?   *on*

What time does it leave?
Mikor indul?   *mi·kawr in·dul*

Please stop here.
Kérem, álljon   *kay·rem aall·yawn*
meg itt.   *meg itt*

Is this taxi available?
Szabad ez a taxi?   *so·bod ez o tok·si*

Behind the Scenes

Send Us Your Feedback

We love to hear from travellers – your comments help make our books better. We read every word, and we guarantee that your feedback goes straight to the authors. Visit **lonelyplanet.com/contact** to submit your updates and suggestions.

Note: We may edit, reproduce and incorporate your comments in Lonely Planet products such as guidebooks, websites and digital products, so let us know if you don't want your comments reproduced or your name acknowledged. For a copy of our privacy policy visit lonelyplanet.com/privacy.

Steve's Thanks

In Budapest, thanks to Bea Szirti, Judit Maróthy and faithful correspondent Virág Vántora for their very helpful suggestions. Gábor and Carolyn Banfalvi and Péter Lengyel showed me the correct wine roads to follow; Tony Láng and Balázs Váradi the political paths. Once again, Michael Buurman opened his flat, conveniently located next to the Great Synagogue; co-author Anna Kaminski was a pleasurable dining companion. A tip of the hat to Zsuzsi Fábián in Kecskemét for help and hospitality. *Nagyon szépen köszönöm mindenkinek!* As always, I'd like to dedicate my share of this to partner Michael Rothschild, with love and gratitude.

Anna's Thanks

A big thank you to Brana, for entrusting me with the most beguiling parts of Hungary, to fellow scribe Steve for all the help and advice on the road, and to everyone who helped me along the way. In particular: András Török, Sándor, Virag, Gabor, Petra, and Julia in Budapest, Kimo and family for the repeated warm welcome in Sopron, the awesome paddleboarding outfit on Lake Balaton and Matthias in Pécs.

Acknowledgements

Cover Photograph: Fishermen's Bastion, Luigi Vaccarella/4Corners ©

This Book

This 2nd edition of Lonely Planet's *Pocket Budapest* guidebook was researched and written by Steve Fallon and Anna Kaminski. The previous edition was written by Steve Fallon. This guidebook was produced by the following:

Curator Anne Mason

Destination Editor Brana Vladisavljevic

Product Editor Genna Patterson

Senior Cartographer David Kemp

Book Designer Gwen Cotter

Assisting Editors Imogen Bannister, Nigel Chin, Katie Connolly, Victoria Harrison Gabrielle Stefanos

Cover Researcher Naomi Parker

Thanks to Santiago Cepeda, Liz Heynes, Camilla Jensen, Andi Jones, Sandie Kestell, Alf Menzies, Lauren O'Connell, Martine Power, Av Rivel, Jessica Ryan, Ellie Simpson, Angela Tinson, Tony Wheeler, Juan Winata

ndex

See also separate subindexes for:

⊗ **Eating p157**

☕ **Drinking p158**

✪ **Entertainment p158**

🛍 **Shopping p158**

Our Writers

Steve Fallon

A native of Boston, Massachusetts, Steve graduated from Georgetown University with a BS in Modern languages. After working for an American daily newspaper and earning an MA in Journalism, his fascination with the 'new' Asia led him to Hong Kong, for over a dozen years, working for a variety of media and running his own travel bookshop. Steve lived in Budapest for three years before moving to London in 1994. He has written or contributed to more than 100 Lonely Planet titles.

Anna Kaminski

Soviet-born, Anna finds a lot to appreciate about Hungary, a country she first visited as a dental tourist in the early 2000s and has been drawn back to since – from the familiar relics of Communism to the world's best poppy-seed strudel. The latest research stint took her from the art galleries and palaces along the Danube and Lake Balaton's shores to Budapest's graveyards; she trawled the latter for her great-uncle who died during the Siege of Budapest.

Published by Lonely Planet Global Limited
CRN 554153
2nd edition – July 2017
ISBN 978 1 786 5702 84
© Lonely Planet 2017 Photographs © as indicated 2017
10 9 8 7 6 5 4 3 2 1
Printed in Malaysia